D1615106

n.a., "Untitled," n.d., photograph card, 4.125 x 2 in. Published by Richard Smith, London. Held at The Spurgeon Library, Midwestern Baptist Theological Seminary, Kansas City, Missouri.

"THE SUM AND SUBSTANCE OF THE GOSPEL"

The Christ-Centered Piety of
Charles Haddon Spurgeon

Introduced and Edited by
Nathan A. Finn and
Aaron Lumpkin

Reformation Heritage Books
Grand Rapids, Michigan

"The Sum and Substance of the Gospel"
© 2020 by Nathan A. Finn and Aaron Lumpkin

All rights reserved. No part of this book may be used or reproduced in any manner whatsoever without written permission except in the case of brief quotations embodied in critical articles and reviews. Direct your requests to the publisher at the following address:

Reformation Heritage Books
2965 Leonard St. NE
Grand Rapids, MI 49525
616-977-0889
orders@heritagebooks.org
www.heritagebooks.org

Printed in the United States of America
20 21 22 23 24 25/10 9 8 7 6 5 4 3 2 1

Library of Congress Cataloging-in-Publication Data

Names: Spurgeon, C. H. (Charles Haddon), 1834-1892, author. |
   Finn, Nathan A., editor. | Lumpkin, Aaron, editor.
Title: "The sum and substance of the Gospel" : the Christ-centered
   piety of Charles Haddon Spurgeon / introduced and edited by
   Nathan A. Finn and Aaron Lumpkin.
Description: Grand Rapids, Michigan : Reformation Heritage Books,
   [2020] | Series: Profiles in Reformed spirituality | Includes biblio-
   graphical references.
Identifiers: LCCN 2020002634 (print) | LCCN 2020002635 (ebook)
   | ISBN 9781601786838 (paperback) | ISBN 9781601786845
   (epub)
Subjects: LCSH: Piety. | Spirituality—Christianity.
Classification: LCC BV4647.P5 S68 2020 (print) | LCC BV4647.P5
   (ebook) | DDC 230.092—dc23
LC record available at https://lccn.loc.gov/2020002634
LC ebook record available at https://lccn.loc.gov/2020002635

For additional Reformed literature, request a free book list from Reformation Heritage Books at the above regular or e-mail address.

PROFILES IN REFORMED SPIRITUALITY
series editors—Joel R. Beeke and Michael A. G. Haykin

Table of Contents

Profiles in Reformed Spirituality

Charles Dickens's famous line in *A Tale of Two Cities*— "It was the best of times, it was the worst of times" —seems well suited to Western evangelicalism since the 1960s. On the one hand, these decades have seen much for which to praise God and to rejoice. In His goodness and grace, for instance, Reformed truth is no longer a house under siege. Growing numbers identify themselves theologically with what we hold to be biblical truth, namely, Reformed theology and piety. And yet, as an increasing number of Reformed authors have noted, there are many sectors of the surrounding western evangelicalism that are characterized by great shallowness and a trivialization of the weighty things of God. So much of evangelical worship seems barren. And when it comes to spirituality, there is little evidence of the riches of our heritage as Reformed evangelicals.

As it was at the time of the Reformation, when the watchword was *ad fontes*—"back to the sources"—so it is now: The way forward is backward. We need to go back to the spiritual heritage of Reformed evangelicalism to find the pathway forward. We cannot live in the past; to attempt to do so would be antiquarianism. But our Reformed forebearers in the faith can teach us much about Christianity, its doctrines, its passions, and its fruit.

And they can serve as our role models. As R. C. Sproul has noted of such giants as Augustine, Martin Luther, John Calvin, and Jonathan Edwards: "These men all were conquered, overwhelmed, and spiritually intoxicated by their vision of the holiness of God. Their minds and imaginations were captured by the majesty of God the Father. Each of them possessed a profound affection for the sweetness and excellence of Christ. There was in each of them a singular and unswerving loyalty to Christ that spoke of a citizenship in heaven that was always more precious to them than the applause of men."[1]

To be sure, we would not dream of placing these men and their writings alongside the Word of God. John Jewel (1522–1571), the Anglican apologist, once stated: "What say we of the fathers, Augustine, Ambrose, Jerome, Cyprian?... They were learned men, and learned fathers; the instruments of the mercy of God, and vessels full of grace. We despise them not, we read them, we reverence them, and give thanks unto God for them. Yet...we may not make them the foundation and warrant of our conscience: we may not put our trust in them. Our trust is in the name of the Lord."[2]

Seeking, then, both to honor the past and yet not idolize it, we are issuing these books in the series Profiles in Reformed Spirituality. The design is to introduce the spirituality and piety of the Reformed

---

1. R. C. Sproul, "An Invaluable Heritage," *Tabletalk* 23, no. 10 (October 1999): 5–6.

2. Cited in Barrington R. White, "Why Bother with History?," *Baptist History and Heritage* 4, no. 2 (July 1969): 85.

tradition by presenting descriptions of the lives of notable Christians with select passages from their works. This combination of biographical sketches and collected portions from primary sources gives a taste of the subjects' contributions to our spiritual heritage and some direction as to how the reader can find further edification through their works. It is the hope of the publisher that this series will provide riches for those areas where we are poor and light of day where we are stumbling in the deepening twilight.

—Joel R. Beeke
Michael A. G. Haykin

Acknowledgments

As with any writing project, there were numerous individuals who helped bring this book to fruition. We want to begin by thanking Michael Haykin, the series coeditor who first expressed interest in this project, and Jay Collier, the director of publishing, who remained interested in this project when it became bogged down due to a variety of distractions in both our lives. Jay especially was willing to periodically remind us that we needed to "land the plane," and we likely would never have completed this book without his gentle prodding. Our wives and children have patiently and graciously endured early mornings, late nights, and busy weekends as we have gathered, edited, and written the various portions of this book. We could not be more thankful for our godly wives, Leah Finn and Sara Lumpkin, as well as our wonderful children.

During our work on this book, we have each been part of institutions that are supportive of our call to research and write for the sake of both the church and the academy. For three years I (Nathan) served as dean of the School of Theology and Missions at Union University, which is a delightful community of academic disciples where this sort of book is celebrated. In the final days of the project, I became

provost and dean of the university faculty at North
Greenville University, which is an institution that
in many ways embodies the sort of Christ-centered
piety in which Spurgeon would have delighted.

I (Aaron) began this project as one of the pastors
of Imago Dei Church in Raleigh, North Carolina,
a Baptist congregation that is uniquely interested
in supporting the ministry of research and writing
because of its close proximity to Southeastern Baptist
Theological Seminary. I now serve as campus minister at Missouri Baptist University, where I spend
much of my time discipling students and cultivating
a spiritual atmosphere conducive to Christ-centered
piety. We are grateful for our colleagues in each of
these places.

We are both proud graduates of Southeastern
Baptist Theological Seminary, which under President
Danny Akin's leadership is training a generation of
pastors and other ministry leaders to own the Great
Commission and make its call to global disciple-
making the center of their ministry. I (Nathan)
served as a faculty member at Southeastern for many
years and continue to teach part-time in the school's
PhD program. I (Aaron) have taught at Southeastern adjunctively and am working on my PhD under
Nathan's supervision. From these vantage points,
we have witnessed firsthand the fruit of President
Akin's leadership. Like us, he does not always agree
with every point of Spurgeon's theology, nor does
Southeastern use Spurgeon's name as much as some
of its sister seminaries. Nevertheless, we believe
Southeastern is the sort of seminary that Spurgeon
would have delighted in, and this is in no small part

because of President Akin's vision for the school. Danny Akin is a godly husband, a loving father and grandfather, a devoted churchman, a gifted preacher and theologian, an exemplary leader, a tireless missions advocate, and a beloved mentor. We dedicate this book to him, with thankfulness to God for his life and ministry.

Russell & Sons, "C. H. Spurgeon," n.d., photograph card, 4.125 x 2 in. Published by Russel & Sons, London. Held at The Spurgeon Library, Midwestern Baptist Theological Seminary, Kansas City, Missouri.

The Life and Piety of Charles Haddon Spurgeon (1834–1892)

According to the late evangelical theologian Carl F. H. Henry (1913–2003), "Charles Haddon Spurgeon is one of evangelical Christianity's immortals."[1] Spurgeon was one of the best-known pastors in church history and perhaps the most famous preacher of the modern era. During his lifetime, he pastored the largest Protestant church in the world: the Metropolitan Tabernacle in London. His preaching attracted believers and skeptics from every walk of life in a context where Dissenters from the established Church of England were considered to be of a lower social class. His published sermons were read all over the English-speaking world and continue to provide spiritual nourishment to present-day believers. Most of his almost 140 books were best sellers when they were published, and many of them are still read today.

Contemporary Christians honor Spurgeon's name in many ways. In England, at least two Baptist churches are named in Spurgeon's honor.[2] In

---

1. Carl F. H. Henry, foreword to Lewis Drummond, *Spurgeon: Prince of Preachers* (Grand Rapids: Kregel, 1992), 11.

2. Spurgeon Baptist Church in Bletchley, Milton Keynes, Buckinghamshire and Spurgeon Memorial Baptist Church on the island of Guernsey.

the American Midwest, an association of Calvinistic Southern Baptist churches is named after the preacher.[3] Several American seminaries own aspects of Spurgeon's legacy. For several years, Reformed Theological Seminary (RTS) in Orlando, Florida, hosted an annual Spurgeon Lecture Series dedicated to Calvinistic Baptist life, thought, and ministry, while Western Seminary in Portland, Oregon, sponsors a minister's fraternal named the Spurgeon Fellowship.[4] Spurgeon's name is especially identified with Midwestern Baptist Theological Seminary in Kansas City, which houses his personal library, sponsors an annual lecture as part of their Spurgeon Center for Biblical Preaching, and renamed their undergraduate program Spurgeon College.[5] Anecdotally, one still regularly finds young men named "Charles Spurgeon," "Spurgeon," or even "Haddon" in honor of the famed preacher.

Not surprisingly, Spurgeon remains an especially beloved figure among pastors, where esteem for him reaches across a variety of boundaries. Though a Baptist, his enduring popularity transcends his own ecclesial tradition. Though a Calvinist, he is

---

3. For more on the Spurgeon Baptist Association of Churches, see http://sbaoc.org/.

4. The Spurgeon Lecture Series at RTS was part of the school's Nicole Institute of Baptist Studies, which is no longer active at the time of this writing. See https://www.thegospelcoalition.org/blogs/justin-taylor/the-nicole-institute-of-baptist-studies-at-rts-orlando/. For more on the Spurgeon Fellowship at Western Seminary, see http://www.thespurgeonfellowship.org/.

5. For more on Midwestern's Spurgeon Center, see http://spurgeoncenter.com/.

appreciated by many Arminians and others who would differ with his view of God's sovereignty. Though an Englishman, Spurgeon is admired well beyond the British Isles and even outside the English-speaking world. He has been called the "Prince of Preachers" and the "heir of the Puritans."[6] Many fundamentalists claim Spurgeon as one of their own, or at least a forerunner, because of his separation from the Baptist Union during the Downgrade Controversy.[7] Though there is much to appreciate about Spurgeon, the purpose of this book is to hold him forth as a model of Christ-centered piety as evidenced in his preaching, his voluminous writings, and even his personal correspondence.

Early Life and Ministry

Charles Spurgeon was born June 19, 1834, to John and Eliza Spurgeon in the English village of Kelvedon in Essex. When Charles was around eighteen months old, due to economic hardship his parents

6. See Drummond, *Spurgeon: Prince of Preachers*; Richard Ellsworth Day, *The Shadow of the Broad Brim: The Life Story of Charles Haddon Spurgeon, Heir of the Puritans* (Philadelphia, Pa.: Judson, 1934); and Ernest W. Bacon, *Spurgeon: Heir of the Puritans* (Grand Rapids: Eerdmans, 1968).

7. See George M. Marsden, "Fundamentalism as an American Phenomenon, A Comparison with English Evangelicalism," in *Fundamentalism and Evangelicalism*, vol. 10, *Modern American Protestantism and Its World*, ed. Mary E. Marty (Berlin, Germany: Walter de Gruyter, 1993), 44–45. For Spurgeon's influence on British Baptist fundamentalism, see David Bebbington, "Baptists and Fundamentalism in Inter-War Britain," in *Evangelicalism and Fundamentalism in the United Kingdom during the Twentieth Century* (New York: Oxford University Press, 2013), 95–114.

sent him to live with his paternal grandparents in the nearby village of Stambourne. His grandfather James Spurgeon pastored the Independent church in Stambourne for fifty-four years. The Independents were a Dissenting tradition with roots in the Congregationalist wing of the Puritan movement. James owned an extensive library that included many Puritan works; this library proved helpful to Charles during his formative years. Charles was something of a prodigy, and by the age of five or six he was already reading works such as *Foxe's Book of Martyrs* and *Pilgrim's Progress* and reading publicly as part of family worship in his grandparents' home.[8]

After five years with his grandparents, Charles moved back in with his parents, who by this time had relocated to the larger town of Colchester. John Spurgeon was employed as a clerk in a coal merchant's office and was serving as pastor of the Independent church in the nearby village of Tollesbury. Charles continued to spend summers with his grandparents, where he made use of James's library by reading works by Puritan theologians and other Reformed authors. Though godly parents and grandparents had reared Charles in devoutly Christian homes, he was not yet converted by his early teenage years.

In 1849, at age fifteen, Charles began attending a local academy in the village of Newmarket. By this time, he was wrestling with his sin and need for salvation, influenced by Puritan evangelistic writers such as Richard Baxter and Joseph Alleine. While

---

8. Arnold Dallimore, *Spurgeon: A New Biography* (Edinburgh: Banner of Truth, 1985), 6.

traveling back home from Newmarket to Colchester in December 1849, Charles stopped at a Primitive Methodist chapel and was convicted by the sermon. The text was from Isaiah 45:22, "Look unto me, and be ye saved, all the ends of the earth." Spurgeon recounted his conversion testimony many times, most famously as recorded in his autobiography.[9] Spurgeon's life was radically altered on that day when he turned from his sin and trusted Jesus Christ as his Lord and Savior.

Spurgeon was not destined to remain an Independent; a few months after his conversion, he became convinced that baptism was for believers only. In May 1850, Spurgeon was baptized by a Particular Baptist minister in the village of Isleham and became a member of that congregation, somewhat to his parents' chagrin. According to Spurgeon, his mother later remarked of his baptism, "Ah, Charles! I often prayed the Lord to make you a Christian, but I never asked that you might become a Baptist." He responded playfully, "Ah, mother! the Lord answered your prayer with His usual bounty, and given you exceeding abundantly above what you

---

9. *The Autobiography of Charles H. Spurgeon, Compiled from His Life, Letters, and Records by His Wife and Private Secretary* (London: Passmore and Alabaster, 1897–1900), 1:105–8. Peter Morden recently questioned whether or not all the details of Spurgeon's conversion testimony are factually accurate, noting inconsistencies in various recountings. Nevertheless, Morden agreed Spurgeon's conversion was a signal event in his life and dramatically influenced his own spirituality. See Peter J. Morden, *Communion with Christ and His People: The Spirituality of C. H. Spurgeon* (Eugene, Ore.: Pickwick, 2013), 50–55.

Primitive Methodist Chapel

C. H. Spurgeon, C. H. Spurgeon's Autobiography. Compiled from His Diary, Letters, and Records. Vol. 1. 4 vols (London: Passmore and Alabaster, 1897), 107.

asked or thought."[10] Though he had not previously
been familiar with the Baptists, Spurgeon remained
one for the rest of his life.

Spurgeon almost immediately began to teach
Sunday school, where his giftedness for ministry
was first affirmed. That fall, Spurgeon enrolled as a
student-teacher in an academy in Cambridge, where
he joined the St. Andrew's Street Baptist Church.
Soon, he became involved in village preaching, an
itinerant ministry wherein lay preachers shared
the gospel with unbelievers and provided pastoral
care without any sort of chapel for Dissenters in
small villages.[11] Through that ministry, the small
Baptist congregation in the village of Waterbeach
called Spurgeon to be their pastor in October 1851.
Spurgeon resigned from the academy. His formal
schooling was over, though he briefly considered
enrolling in the Baptist-related Stepney College
in London. Spurgeon attempted to meet with the
school's principal, Joseph Angus, at the home of
a mutual acquaintance, but at the appointed time
a maid showed both men to different rooms, pre-
venting them from meeting. Spurgeon interpreted
the maid's error as God providentially leading him
away from formal ministerial education.[12] In the
two years Spurgeon was a pastor in Waterbeach, the

---

10. *Autobiography*, 1:69.

11. For more on village preaching, see Deryck W. Lovegrove,
"Lay Leadership, Establishment Crisis and the Disdain of the
Clergy," in *The Rise of the Laity in Evangelical Protestantism* (New
York: Routledge, 2002), 117–33.

12. Drummond, *Spurgeon*, 171–73.

church experienced steady growth and he developed a reputation as a gifted young preacher.

Pastoral Ministry in London

After Spurgeon preached at a regional Sunday school rally in Cambridge, the New Park Street Chapel in Southwark, London, invited him to fill their pulpit in late 1853. New Park Street was the then-present location of the Particular Baptist congregation that had previously been pastored through the years by such gifted men as Benjamin Keach (served 1672–1704), John Gill (served 1720–1771), and John Rippon (served 1773–1836). Though the church owned a sizable building, in recent years the congregation had dwindled significantly as three different pastors served relatively short stints between 1836 and 1853.[13] After making a good first impression and preaching for a trial period during January 1854, New Park Street Chapel called the nineteen-year-old Spurgeon as their pastor in February of that year. He would remain pastor of the congregation until his death in 1892.

Though New Park Street's large sanctuary included twelve hundred seats, soon the meeting-house was not sufficient to accommodate the massive crowds who were coming to hear Spurgeon preach. The sanctuary was expanded about two years after Spurgeon arrived, but even with two thousand seats

---

13. Drummond estimated the attendance at no more than eighty, while Tom Nettles suggested it may have been closer to two hundred. See Drummond, *Spurgeon*, 189; and Tom Nettles, *Living by Revealed Truth: The Life and Pastoral Theology of Charles Haddon Spurgeon* (Fearn, Ross-shire, Scotland: Christian Focus, 2013), 70.

now available, the building still was not nearly big enough. During renovations Spurgeon preached at Exeter Hall in the Strand in north London, a large venue with four thousand seats; the crowds exceeded even this sizable capacity. In 1856, the church began constructing a new meetinghouse, and in the interim the congregation met at the newly constructed Surrey Gardens Music Hall on Sunday morning, where almost six thousand people heard Spurgeon preach every week. In October 1857, Spurgeon preached to almost twenty-four thousand people at a special national Fast Day service held in the Crystal Palace, the largest venue in London. One biographer suggests this might be the largest single congregation gathered for the preaching of the gospel up to that point in history.[14]

It was during this season that Spurgeon faced one of his first great trials. On October 19, 1856, during a packed evening service at the Music Hall, someone yelled there was a fire in the building and the galleries were collapsing—but this was not true. Seven people died and twenty-eight others were seriously injured due to trampling as the crowd ran for the exits to escape the nonexistent fire. The papers mercilessly blamed Spurgeon, which drove him into a deep depression that caused him not to preach the following Sunday and even consider leaving the ministry. Fortunately, the Lord brought him out of his depression and gave Spurgeon a renewed sense of pastoral calling. When he returned to the pulpit

---

14. Bacon, *Spurgeon*, 53.

on November 2, he expressed his resolve to press on by faith:

> God forgive those who were instigators of that horrid act! They have my forgiveness from the depths of my soul. *It shall not stop us, however;* we are not in the least degree daunted by it. I shall preach there [the Music Hall] yet again; aye, and God will give us souls there, and Satan's empire shall tremble more than ever. God is with us; who is he that shall be against us?[15]

In March 1861, Spurgeon's church moved into its new meetinghouse in the Elephant and Castle neighborhood in South London, near the River Thames. The new building included seating for about forty-five hundred and standing space for another thousand worshipers. The congregation was renamed the Metropolitan Tabernacle. Within months of Spurgeon's ministry at the Metropolitan Tabernacle, the membership grew from 313 to over two thousand, hundreds of whom joined by baptism. The membership was almost three thousand by 1864.[16] Long before the term *megachurch* came into common parlance, Spurgeon pastored a gigantic congregation in a major urban center. This remarkable growth would continue throughout his pastoral career. By the end of his thirty-seven-year ministry, the Metropolitan Tabernacle had baptized 14,460

---

15. *Autobiography*, 2:214.
16. These membership statistics can be found in Drummond, *Spurgeon*, 208–9.

individuals and the church's membership stood at over five thousand.[17]

Ministerial Entrepreneur

Many pastors are gifted preachers, but Spurgeon's ministry was marked by far more than simply a pronounced homiletical aptitude. He was a remarkably creative pastor who used his pastoral labors at the Metropolitan Tabernacle as a launching pad for a larger ministry of teaching, theological education, and mercy ministries. In this way, Spurgeon anticipated later Reformed and evangelical ministers who would establish significant personal ministries that extended their ministry to their local congregation.

In 1855, Spurgeon began to publish his sermons in periodicals, which were transcribed on Sundays and edited by Spurgeon himself the following morning. On Tuesdays, the sermons were reprinted in periodicals all over the English-speaking world. Arnold Dallimore claimed Spurgeon published a new sermon every week until his death.[18] At the conclusion of each year, his sermons were bound together in volumes that are still available under the titles *The New Park Street Pulpit* and *The Metropolitan Tabernacle Pulpit*. Numerous other shorter thematic anthologies of his sermons were also published, both before and after his death. In 1865, Spurgeon began to publish a monthly magazine titled *The Sword*

---

17. David W. Bebbington, *The Dominance of Evangelicalism: The Age of Spurgeon and Moody*, A History of Evangelicalism: People, Movements and Ideas in the English-Speaking World (Downers Grove, Ill.: IVP Academic, 2005), 41.

18. Dallimore, *Spurgeon*, 191.

and the Trowel, which helped to build his following among like-minded Baptists and other evangelicals. Tom Nettles suggested *The Sword and the Trowel* was Spurgeon's chief means of weekly contact with like-minded friends and even his parishioners.[19] He also wrote numerous letters during his adult life, many of which were subsequently included in his four-volume *Autobiography* (1897–1900), edited by his wife, Susannah, after Spurgeon's death.

In addition to his published collections of sermons, Spurgeon also had an extensive book-writing ministry. He authored dozens of books during the course of his ministry, and many others were compiled after his death. His more famous books include *Morning by Morning* (1865), *Evening by Evening* (1868), *John Ploughman's Talks* (1868), *The Treasury of David* (1870), *Lectures to My Students* (1875), *Commenting and Commentaries* (1876), *All of Grace* (1892), *The Soul Winner* (1895), *Till He Come: Communion Meditations and Addresses* (1896), and *Grace Triumphant* (1904). Nearly all his books were published by one of his church's deacons, Joseph Passmore, and his business partner James Alabaster. A decade after Spurgeon's death, one biographer estimated Spurgeon's printed sermons alone contained between 200 and 300 million words.[20] Almost a century later, another biographer suggested Spurgeon had more religious books in print than any other English-speaking author.[21] Today,

---

19. Nettles, *Living by Revealed Truth*, 399.

20. Charles Ray, *The Life of Charles Haddon Spurgeon* (London: Passmore and Alabaster, 1903), 449.

21. Drummond, *Spurgeon*, 25, 315.

through the work of evangelical and Reformed publishers, reprint companies, and the internet, nearly all of Spurgeon's books remain available.

In 1856, Spurgeon opened the Pastor's College, a church-based training academy for (mostly) Baptist ministers who could give a clear Christian testimony and already had some preaching experience. Though he did not have a college education himself, Spurgeon taught classes in pastoral ministry at the college; many of his lectures were later published as part of the book *Lectures to My Students.* Between 1856 and 1892, the Pastor's College trained almost nine hundred men, nearly all of whom remained stoutly conservative, evangelical, Calvinistic Baptists into the early twentieth century. Ten men who graduated during Spurgeon's tenure at the college went on to serve as president of the Baptist Union prior to World War I, while alumni served in churches in many other nations including the United States, Canada, Australia, New Zealand, India, as well as various stations in the West Indies, and South Africa.[22] Today, the school is named Spurgeon's College and continues to train men and women for the evangelical ministry, especially in churches affiliated with the Baptist Union of Great Britain.[23]

Contemporary evangelicals debate the place of mercy ministries and social justice in gospel ministry. Like many evangelicals of his era, Spurgeon's

---

22. Bebbington, *The Dominance of Evangelicalism*, 45.

23. For a recent history of Spurgeon's College, see Ian M. Randall, *A School of the Prophets: 150 Years of Spurgeon's College* (London: Spurgeon's College, 2005).

vision of faithful ministry encompassed both evangelism and benevolence, each of which was considered
essential to faithful ministry.[24] He also founded two
different orphanages as a way to combat one of the
Victorian era's major social ills. In 1867, the church
opened the Stockwell Orphanage for boys; twelve
years later, in 1879, a girl's wing was added to the
orphanage. Spurgeon also inherited an almshouse
ministry that had been established during John
Rippon's ministry at the church. The almshouse
provided free housing, food, and clothing for needy
widows who were members of the Metropolitan Tabernacle. It also operated a school for needy children
who could not afford to attend a costly private school
(England offered no state-sponsored education at
the time). The church's widows served as teachers
at the school. In 1875, Susannah Spurgeon began a
book fund to provide the poor students at the Pastor's College with a sufficient pastoral library. Many
present-day collegians and seminary students no
doubt wish for a revival of Susannah's book fund!

Baptist, Calvinist, Evangelical

Spurgeon was a committed Baptist from almost the
beginning of his Christian life and remained convinced of so-called Baptist distinctives throughout
his ministry. He was a particularly strong proponent
of believer's baptism, which he believed was a public profession of faith, a key act of discipleship, an
important symbol of the gospel truth, and a necessary

---

24. Bebbington, *The Dominance of Evangelicalism*, 99; and Nettles,
Living by Revealed Truth, 340.

prerequisite to church membership.[25] Spurgeon was especially concerned with any views of infant baptism that he believed implied baptismal regeneration. For example, in 1864 Spurgeon preached a sermon titled "Baptismal Regeneration" that became arguably his most famous and controversial sermon. He argued that the Church of England's official position was baptismal regeneration, which he considered a popish doctrine.[26] He preached this message at a time when the High Church Tractarians associated with the Oxford Movement were trying to move the Church of England closer to Rome and when several leading Anglican clergymen such as John Henry Newman were converting to Catholicism.[27]

Though a committed Baptist, Spurgeon was also a staunch Calvinist at a time when traditional Reformed theology was becoming less popular among historically Calvinistic Dissenters.[28] Many in Spurgeon's own Particular Baptist tradition, embodied in the Baptist Union (established 1813), were

25. The best introduction to Spurgeon's baptismal views is Morden, *Communion with Christ and His People*, 77–103.

26. See "Baptismal Regeneration," which is available as appendix B in Drummond, *Spurgeon*, 787–802.

27. For more on the Oxford Movement, see C. Brad Faught, *The Oxford Movement: A Thematic History of the Tractarians and Their Times* (University Park: Penn State University Press, 2004).

28. Spurgeon's Calvinism is acknowledged by nearly all historians and is a major theme in Nettles, *Living by Revealed Truth*. See also Iain H. Murray, *The Forgotten Spurgeon* (Edinburgh: Banner of Truth, 1978); Robert W. Oliver, *History of the English Calvinistic Baptists, 1771–1892: From John Gill to C. H. Spurgeon* (Edinburgh: Banner of Truth, 2006), 337–56; and Morden, *Communion with Christ and His People*, 16–46.

softening their views on election and embracing general atonement.[29] In the years 1832, 1863, and 1873, the Baptist Union was either reorganized or the terms of cooperation were revised to allow for greater theological diversity and to encourage the historically Arminian General Baptists to participate in the Baptist Union.[30] In 1855, just a year after arriving at the New Park Street Church, Spurgeon republished a lightly revised version of the Second London Confession. This confession, which had been written in 1677 and was publicly adopted in 1689, had fallen into disuse among Particular Baptists, including those who continued to maintain a commitment to a Reformed view of salvation. Also in 1855, Spurgeon prepared a catechism that drew on the Westminster Shorter Catechism (1647) and the so-called Baptist Catechism (1677). Spurgeon also evidenced his Reformed theology in his preaching ministry, many of his articles in *The Sword and the Trowel*, and in several of his books.

Spurgeon appreciated the ministry of his pastoral predecessor John Gill, a respected but controversial

---

29. Though many contemporaries blamed this transition on Andrew Fuller, the key figure in the softening of Particular Baptist Calvinism was Robert Hall Jr. (1764–1831). For a recent discussion of Hall's theological transition vis-à-vis election and the atonement, see Cody Heath McNutt, "The Ministry of Robert Hall, Jr.: The Preacher as Theological Exemplar and Cultural Celebrity" (PhD diss., Southern Baptist Theological Seminary, 2012), 110–16.

30. See Roger Hayden, *English Baptist History and Heritage* (Didcot, Oxfordshire, U.K.: Baptist Union of Great Britain, 2005), 144–46.

figure whom many identified with hyper-Calvinism.[31] However, Spurgeon personally resonated more with the seventeenth-century Puritan authors he had first discovered in his grandfather's library and the emphases associated with Fullerism, an evangelical renewal movement among the Particular Baptists named for Andrew Fuller (1754–1815).[32] Like Fuller before him, Spurgeon's evangelical Calvinism drew the ire of both Arminians, who did not agree with his Calvinism, and hyper-Calvinists, who did not agree with Spurgeon's commitment to evangelistic preaching. Though Fullerism had crippled the influence of hyper-Calvinism among most Calvinistic Baptists, a minority of "Strict and Particular Baptists" continued to embrace hyper-Calvinist sentiments and refused to cooperate with the Baptist Union because they judged it to be influenced by Fullerism, which they considered a declension from historic Calvinism.[33] Spurgeon and Baptist hyper-Calvinists

---

31. For varying perspectives on Gill's alleged hyper-Calvinism, see the essays in Michael A. G. Haykin, ed., *The Life and Thought of John Gill (1697–1771): A Tercentennial Appreciation* (New York: Brill, 1997).

32. See G. Stephen Weaver, "C. H. Spurgeon: A Fullerite?," *Journal of Baptist Studies* 8 (2016): 99–117. For a recent study of Fuller, see Peter J. Morden, *The Life and Thought of Andrew Fuller (1754–1815)*, Studies in Evangelical History and Thought (Bletchley, Milton Keynes, U.K.: Paternoster, 2015).

33. Strict Communion, the practice of restricting the Lord's Supper to those who have experienced believer's baptism, also factored in to the growing divide. The key studies of the Strict and Particular Baptists are Kenneth Dix, *Strict and Particular: English Strict and Particular Baptists in the Nineteenth Century* (Didcot, Oxfordshire, U.K.: Baptist Historical Society, 2001); and Geoffrey R. Breed, *Particular*

engaged in heated debates about how the doctrines such as election, effectual calling, and particular atonement should relate to evangelism, conversion, and the Christian life.[34]

In addition to his Baptist beliefs and his Calvinist convictions, Spurgeon was also active in broader evangelical circles beyond his own denomination, in part because of his commitment to evangelical activism.[35] Though he was a strong critic of Arminian

---

Baptists in Victorian England and Their Strict Communion Organizations (Didcot, Oxfordshire, U.K.: Baptist Historical Society, 2003). See also Oliver, *History of the English Calvinistic Baptists*, 260–336. Today, many Strict and Particular Baptists adhere to an evangelical Calvinism that is closer to Spurgeon's views.

34. For a fine study of Spurgeon's controversy with hyper-Calvinists, see Iain H. Murray, *Spurgeon v. Hyper-Calvinism: The Battle for Gospel Preaching* (Edinburgh: Banner of Truth, 1995). Interestingly, while Spurgeon was deeply critical of High Calvinism, he did not believe Gill was a consistent hyper-Calvinist. In his autobiography, Spurgeon said of Gill,

> The system of theology with which many identify his name has chilled many churches to their very soul, for it has led them to omit the free invitations of the gospel, and to deny that it is the duty of sinners to believe in Jesus; but for this, Dr. Gill must not be altogether held responsible, for a candid reader of his Commentary will soon perceive in it expressions altogether out of accord with such a narrow system; and it is well known that, when he was dealing with practical godliness, he was so bold in his utterances that the devotees of Hyper-Calvinism could not endure him. "Well sir," said one of these, "if I had not been told that it was the great Dr. Gill who preached, I should have said I had heard an Arminian."

See *Autobiography*, 1:310.

35. See Drummond, *Spurgeon*, 393–441. For broader historical context related to interdenominational cooperation among

theology, Spurgeon was friendly with a number of Arminian pastors. As long as Arminians remained committed to evangelical doctrines such as justification by faith alone and penal substitutionary atonement, Spurgeon saw them as erring but genuine brothers in Christ. Though he was critical of infant baptism and episcopal polity, Spurgeon maintained friendships with evangelical paedobaptists and partnered with them in pan-evangelical initiatives. George Rogers, a Congregationalist minister, served as the first principal of Spurgeon's Pastor's College, despite the two men's differing views of baptism. Spurgeon invited many prominent non-Baptist evangelicals to preach at the Metropolitan Tabernacle, including D. L. Moody (1837–1899) and A. T. Pierson (1837–1911). The latter, a Presbyterian at the time, supplied the pulpit on a weekly basis during the final months of Spurgeon's life and for several months after his death. Against earlier Baptist practice but reflecting a growing trend among nineteenth-century British Baptists, Spurgeon also practiced open Communion by inviting paedobaptists to celebrate the Lord's Supper at the Metropolitan Tabernacle.[36]

Though part of an ecclesial tradition that has at times been marked by sectarianism, Spurgeon

---

evangelicals in the Victorian era, see Bebbington, *The Dominance of Evangelicalism*, 82–116.

36. See Timothy George, "Controversy and Communion: The Limits of Baptist Fellowship from Bunyan to Spurgeon," in *The Gospel and the World: International Baptist Studies*, Studies in Baptist History and Thought, ed. David W. Bebbington (Carlisle, Cumbria, England: Paternoster, 2002), 55–57.

exemplified a Reformed and evangelical catholicity. Though deeply theological, like the great Methodist evangelist George Whitefield (1714–1770), Spurgeon emphasized the common experience of regeneration more than the doctrinal (and especially ecclesiological) convictions of the regenerate. What this meant in practice was that Spurgeon appreciated the universal church to a greater degree than many of his fellow Baptists. Spurgeon remained committed to a Baptist view of the local church, though he did not think denominational distinctives undermined the essential unity of all those who have been regenerated. He is a role model for contemporary believers who wish to emphasize "gospel-centered" evangelical cooperation among believers from differing denominational traditions.

Faithfulness in Suffering

Spurgeon experienced considerable suffering during his lifetime. For example, Spurgeon periodically battled depression in the years after the aforementioned Surrey Gardens disaster. At times, Spurgeon would be so depressed he would miss several weeks of preaching. At least one biographer suggested Spurgeon's depression ran so deep that he would at times question either his salvation or his fitness for ministry.[37] Peter Morden argued that Spurgeon suffered from both clinical depression and spiritual depression.[38] Because of his own struggles with

---

37. Drummond, *Spurgeon*, 327, 345. See also Dallimore, *Spurgeon*, 226.

38. Morden, *Communion with Christ and His People*, 262.

depression, Spurgeon regularly discussed the topic in his sermons and lectures. Depression, melancholy, and related themes also regularly appear in his autobiography. Spurgeon's depression was such a part of his life and he addressed it so frequently that one recent book uses Spurgeon as a conversation partner for contemporary Christians who battle depression.[39]

Physical suffering frequently exacerbated Spurgeon's depression. He possessed a fairly sickly constitution, so he suffered from frequent illness and regularly battled fatigue; the latter is not surprising in light of how busy he was. Spurgeon's most debilitating physical struggle was with gout; he was in almost constant pain from this malady from 1869 until his death in 1892. As time went on, he would have to be absent from the pulpit as much as three months of each year to recover in a resort town in France. He also struggled with joint and kidney inflammation; both conditions were related to his gout. During the final decade of his life, his congregation often did not know from week to week if Spurgeon would be in the pulpit. As his condition deteriorated during the time of the Downgrade Controversy (to be discussed below), Spurgeon was unable to preach at the Metropolitan Tabernacle for the final six months of his life.

Despite his suffering, Spurgeon remained a mostly happy man who persevered through his trials because he believed the Lord had ordained his sufferings for the sake of his sanctification. In fact,

---

39. See Zack Eswine, *Spurgeon's Sorrows: Realistic Hope for Those Who Suffer from Depression* (Fearn, Ross-shire, Scotland: Christian Focus, 2014).

suffering became a key aspect of Spurgeon's piety. Because of his firm belief in God's sovereignty, Spurgeon believed that suffering was a means of grace that the Lord used to bring believers into closer communion with Christ.[40] Many believers consider Spurgeon to be a role model for Christ-centered endurance of suffering, especially among pastors and other ministers of the gospel. For example, in a recent book John Piper dedicated a chapter to Spurgeon's suffering and identifies several lessons that Spurgeon can teach contemporary pastors about preaching through adversity.[41]

The Downgrade Controversy and Final Years

The aforementioned 1873 reorganization of the Baptist Union paved the way for General Baptists to cooperate more closely with the Particular Baptists. At that time, an earlier requirement that cooperating ministers and churches must "agree in the sentiments usually denominated evangelical" was dropped in favor of a statement emphasizing interpretive liberty, provided that believer baptism by immersion was maintained.[42] Theological conservatives in the Baptist Union were troubled by the trend toward downplaying statements of faith, softening Calvinism, and building bridges with General Baptists. In the years after 1873, these trends were increasingly

---

40. Morden, *Communion with Christ and His People*, 274–77.

41. John Piper, *A Camaraderie of Confidence: The Fruit of Unfailing Faith in the Lives of Charles Spurgeon, George Müller, and Hudson Taylor* (Wheaton, Ill.: Crossway, 2016), 33–62.

42. J. H. Y. Briggs, *The English Baptists of the 19th Century* (Didcot, Oxfordshire, U.K.: Baptist Historical Society, 1994), 172.

seen as evidence of a liberalizing tendency within the Baptist Union.[43]

The General Baptists especially were suspected of liberal tendencies. For much of the eighteenth century, the General Baptist tradition had slowly declined because of the influence of rationalism and the toleration of heresies such as Socinianism, which denied the deity of Christ and the necessity of His atonement. Fortunately, General Baptists experienced their own evangelical awakening under the leadership of Daniel Taylor (1738–1816), a Wesleyan-turned-Baptist who organized a "New Connexion" of General Baptists committed to evangelical doctrine.[44] By the mid-nineteenth century, however, the General Baptists had begun tolerating theological error. In particular, a growing number of Arminian Baptists rejected the full trustworthiness of Scripture (biblical inerrancy) and suggested that some who never hear the gospel might be saved based on how they respond to God's general revelation in nature (inclusivism).

The leading General Baptist of the era was John Clifford (1836–1923), a London pastor who also edited the *General Baptist Magazine*, a weekly denominational periodical.[45] Though Clifford was

---

43. Briggs, *The English Baptists*, 171–98; and Hayden, *English Baptist History and Heritage*, 149–50.

44. See Frank W. Rinaldi, *The Tribe of Dan: The New Connexion of General Baptists 1770–1891: A Study in the Transition from Revival Movement to Established Denomination*, Studies in Baptist History and Thought (Carlisle, Cumbria, England: Paternoster, 2008).

45. For more on Clifford and his thought, see Tom J. Nettles, *The Modern Era*, vol. 3, *The Baptists: Key People Involved in Forming*

a personal friend of Spurgeon and he was willing to cooperate with Calvinists, as time went on Clifford became increasingly liberal, adopting higher critical views of Scripture, advocating Darwinism, rejecting substitutionary atonement, and at least implicitly affirming Universalism. These views were especially problematic because Clifford was also emerging as the most influential English Baptist besides Spurgeon. The two pastors' friendship was put under considerable strain in the late 1880s.

In March 1887, an article in *The Sword and the Trowel* claimed that the Baptist Union was in the midst of a theological and moral "down grade."[46] The cause was a creeping liberalism that was increasingly entertained by the Particular Baptists. Spurgeon did not write the article, but as editor he approved of its publication and subsequently defended it. When the article provoked significant controversy, Spurgeon defended the claim that English Baptists—especially

---

a Baptist Identity (Fearn, Ross-shire, Scotland: Christian Focus, 2007), 57–89; and James Leo Garrett, *Baptist Theology: A Four-Century Study* (Macon, Ga.: Mercer University Press, 2009), 272–77.

46. This article and Spurgeon's subsequent defenses of it are reprinted as appendices C–H in Drummond, *Spurgeon*, 802–34. For more on the Downgrade Controversy, see Nettles, *Living by Revealed Truth*, 541–78. See also Jerry L. Faught, "Baptists and the Bible and the Turn toward Theological Controversy: The Downgrade Controversy, 1887," in *Turning Points in Baptist History: A Festschrift in Honor of Harry Leon McBeth*, ed. Michael E. Williams Sr. and Walter B. Shurden (Macon, Ga.: Mercer University Press, 2008), 249–60; and Christian T. George, "Downgrade: Twenty-First Century Lessons from Nineteenth-Century Baptists," in *The SBC and the 21st Century: Reflection, Renewal & Recommitment*, ed. Jason Allen (Nashville, Tenn.: B&H Academic, 2016), 127–37.

those who were Arminians—were tolerating the view that the Bible contained factual errors and were at least flirting with Unitarianism and Universalism. The stage was set for a denomination-wide controversy between Spurgeon and other conservatives, progressives who advocated more liberal views, and moderates who were willing to tolerate liberalism for the sake of institutional unity.

Spurgeon was harshly criticized by many leading Baptist pastors, including Clifford, while students and graduates with ties to the Pastor's College rallied to Spurgeon's defense.[47] Spurgeon demanded that the Baptist Union adopt a conservative doctrinal statement, but leaders rebuffed his opinions. Denominational leaders believed it was enough to affirm a short, somewhat vague statement that affirmed the gospel, biblical authority (though not inerrancy), and believer's baptism. In October 1887, Spurgeon led the Metropolitan to sever ties with the Baptist Union and the London Baptist Association. The church was now an independent Baptist congregation.

Clifford led a delegation that met with Spurgeon and attempted to woo him back, but Spurgeon could not be convinced; he believed that standing for truth was more important than maintaining friendships if the latter were dependent on theological compromise. In January 1888, the Baptist Union formally censured Spurgeon for being divisive. At that point,

---

47. Ian M. Randall, "Charles Haddon Spurgeon, the Pastors' College and the Downgrade Controversy," in *Discipline and Diversity: Papers Read at the 2005 Summer Meeting and the 2006 Winter Meeting of the Ecclesiastical History Society*, ed. Kate Cooper and Jeremy Gregory (Martlesham, Woodbridge, England: Boydell, 2007), 366–76.

Gravesite

Robert Freidus, *"Charles Spurgeon Mausoleum.* West Norwood Cemetery," April 12, 2019. http://www .victorianweb.org/art/architecture/cemeteries/18.html. Used with permission per website.

a number of other churches, almost all of them led by pastors with close ties to Spurgeon, also withdrew from the Baptist Union. In 1891, the Baptist Union completely absorbed the General Baptist denomination. Spurgeon felt like all his concerns were justified when his fellow Calvinists accepted, without any real criticism, the less conservative Arminians.

Unfortunately, the Downgrade Controversy wreaked havoc on Spurgeon's already shaky health. He found himself able to preach less and less, and during his final couple of years, he spent considerable time in France, where he died in January 1892 at the age of fifty-seven. Following a brief period when A. T. Pierson preached, after filling the pulpit himself for well over a year, Spurgeon's son Thomas was called as the church's new pastor in March 1894. Thomas had been pastoring a congregation in Australia. He served as pastor of the Metropolitan Tabernacle until 1908. Though a capable minister who shared his father's doctrine, the church began to gradually decline under Thomas's leadership. The building was bombed during World War II, and though the facade remains in place, a much smaller sanctuary was built. In recent decades, the church has experienced greater numeric growth and spiritual vitality and at this writing is now a thriving congregation of nearly one thousand worshipers from numerous national backgrounds.

Conclusion: Spurgeon's Christ-Centered Piety

Spurgeon's thought was shaped by his shared commitments to Calvinism, evangelicalism, and the Particular Baptist tradition. Each of these components of his identity shared a deep sense that Jesus Christ and His saving work is the source of our salvation as well as the gospel kindling that fuels spiritual growth and cultivates personal holiness. Much like his Puritan predecessors, Spurgeon was a Christ-centered mystic for whom vital Christian experience was intimately linked to the good news of justification by grace through faith on the basis of Christ's perfectly obedient life, substitutionary atonement, and victorious resurrection. As James Gordon argued, Spurgeon's "love for Jesus and his sense of a presence almost tangible, and visible to faith, is one of the recurring themes in his writing. It was this sense of a living, intimate relationship between his soul and Christ that led one admirer to rank him and Bunyan the two greatest Evangelical mystics."[48] In his excellent recent study of Spurgeon's spirituality, Peter Morden agreed, arguing "Spurgeon's spirituality was thoroughly christocentric, with an overriding stress on communion with Christ."[49]

For this volume, we have selected excerpts from Spurgeon's sermons, writings, and correspondence that highlight his Christ-centered piety. The nature of this book and the series it is part of necessarily place a limit on the number of selections we could include. What Lewis Drummond calls *Christocentricity*—an emphasis on the glories of Jesus Christ, His saving work, and its effects upon the believer—literally saturates almost everything Spurgeon preached and wrote.[50] As mentioned above, Spurgeon has left us a vast literary corpus, and we have barely scratched the surface with this book. Nevertheless, we pray this short volume serves as a helpful and edifying point of entry into Spurgeon's Christ-centered piety.

---

48. James M. Gordon, *Evangelical Spirituality* (London: SPCK, 1991; repr., Eugene, Ore.: Wipf and Stock, 2006), 161. The "admirer" Gordon cited is Robertson Nicoll. See T. H. Darlow, *W. Robertson Nicoll: Life and Letters* (London: Hodder and Stoughton, 1925), 402.

49. Morden, *Communion with Christ and His People*, 14.

50. See Drummond, *Spurgeon*, 288–94.

1

─━•◦(•)◦•━─

The Power of the Gospel[1]

The gospel is to the true believer a thing of power. It is Christ, the power of God. Ay, there is a power in God's gospel beyond all description. Once, I, like Mazeppa,[2] bound on the wild horse of my lust, bound hand and foot, incapable of resistance, was galloping on with hell's wolves behind me, howling for my body and my soul, as their just and lawful prey. There came a mighty band which stopped that wild horse, cut my bands, set me down, and brought me into liberty. Is there power, sir? Ay, there is power, and he who has felt it must acknowledge it. There was a time when I lived in the strong old castle of my sins and rested in my works. There came a trumpeter to the door, and he bade me open it. I with anger chid[3] him from the porch and said he never should enter. There came a goodly personage with loving countenance; His hands were marked with scars,

---

1. From "Christ Crucified," *New Park Street Pulpit* (London: Passmore and Alabaster, 1856), 1:57–58. A sermon on 1 Corinthians 1:23–24 delivered at Exeter Hall on February 11, 1855. All subsequent references to *New Park Street Pulpit* are abbreviated *NPSP*.

2. This is a reference to Byron's poem "Mazeppa" (1819), which narrates a legendary ill-fated love affair between a Ukrainian gentleman named Ivan Mazeppa and a married noblewoman.

3. *Chid* means "to scold."

where nails were driven, and His feet had nail prints too. He lifted up His cross, using it as a hammer; at the first blow the gate of my prejudice shook; at the second it trembled more; at the third down it fell, and in He came, and He said, "Arise, and stand upon thy feet, for I have loved thee with an everlasting love." A thing of power! Ah! It is a thing of power. I have felt it here, in this heart; I have the witness of the Spirit within and know it is a thing of might, because it has conquered me; it has bowed me down.

> His free grace alone, from the first to the last,
> Hath won my affection, and held my soul fast.[4]

The gospel to the Christian is a thing of power. What is it that makes the young man devote himself as a missionary to the cause of God, to leave father and mother, and go into distant lands? It is a thing of power that does it—it is the gospel. What is it that constrains yonder minister, in the midst of the cholera, to climb up that creaking staircase and stand by the bed of some dying creature who has that dire disease? It must be a thing of power which leads him to venture his life; it is love of the cross of Christ which bids him do it. What is that which enables one man to stand up before a multitude of his fellows, though unprepared he may be, but determined that he will speak nothing but Christ and Him crucified? What is it that enables him to cry, like the warhorse of Job in battle, "Aha!" and move glorious in might? It is a thing of power that does it—it is Christ crucified.

---

4. From the first stanza of John Stocker, "Thy Mercy My God" (1776), in the public domain.

And what emboldens that timid female to walk down that dark lane in the wet evening, that she may go and sit beside the victim of a contagious fever? What strengthens her to go through that den of thieves and pass by the profligate[5] and profane? What influences her to enter into that charnel house[6] of death and there sit down and whisper words of comfort? Does gold make her do it? They are too poor to give her gold. Does fame make her do it? She shall never be known nor written among the mighty women of this earth. What makes her do it? Is it love of merit? No, she knows she has no desert[7] before high heaven. What impels her to it? It is the power of the gospel on her heart; it is the cross of Christ; she loves it, and she therefore says—

> Were the whole realm of nature mine.
> That were a present far too small;
> Love so mazing, so divine,
> Demands my soul, my life, my all.[8]

---

5. *Profligate* means "recklessly extravagant, wasteful."

6. A charnel house was a vault used for storing human skeletal remains. Charnel houses were often built near church buildings to house skeletons unearthed while digging graves.

7. *Desert* in this context means "just reward."

8. From the final stanza of Isaac Watts, "When I Survey the Wondrous Cross" (1707), in the public domain.

2

Chosen in Christ[1]

Let us first see what the King Himself has done.

He has honored Him in every work of grace. In the decree of election, the eternal Father chose His people, but He chose them "in Christ." He made "the man Christ Jesus,"[2] the head of election. Watts has well sung—

> "Christ be my first elect," He said,
> Then chose our souls in Christ our Head.[3]

"According," says the apostle, "as he hath chosen us *in him* before the foundation of the world."[4] Every after-manifestation of grace has also been through the man Christ Jesus. When did Isaiah speak most evangelically? When did Ezekiel most sweetly comfort the people of God? When did others of the prophets dart bright flashes of light through the thick darkness of their times? Surely it was only when they spoke of Him who bore our transgressions and by

1. From "What Shall Be Done for Jesus?," *The Sword and the Trowel* (January 1865): 3–4. The article offers a reflection on Esther 6:6. All subsequent references to *The Sword and the Trowel* are abbreviated *ST*.

2. 1 Timothy 2:5.

3. From the second stanza of Isaac Watts, "Jesus, We Bless Thy Father's Name" (1706), in the public domain.

4. Ephesians 1:4, emphasis added.

whose stripes we are healed. In the great work of redemption, God has honored Christ by laying our help upon Him alone, as upon "one that is mighty." He has "exalted one chosen out of the people."[5] In Bozrah's battle no champion must fight but Jesus, and covered with the blood of his foes, no hero must return in stately triumph from Edom but the lonely One who speaks in righteousness, "mighty to save."[6] He trod the winepress alone, and of the people there was none with Him. In redemption there is but one price, found in one hand, paid by one Redeemer, that price of the precious blood, found in the veins of the Savior and paid down by Him upon the accursed tree. In every other act of grace the design of the King is to honor the Lord Jesus. You cannot taste the sweetness of any *doctrine* till you have remembered Christ's connection with it. You are washed from every sin, but how? You have "washed [your] robes, and made them white in the blood of the Lamb."[7] You are sumptuously arrayed from head to foot; you are appareled as the King's sons and daughters, but who is this that has clothed you? Are you not robed in the righteousness of your Lord Jesus Christ? Up to this moment you have been preserved, but now? You are "preserved in Jesus Christ."[8] The Holy Spirit is the author of your sanctification, but what has been the instrument by which He has purified you? He has cleansed you by the water which flowed with the

5. Psalm 89:19.

6. Isaiah 63:1. Bozrah was an ancient biblical city, near the modern city of Bouseira, Jordan.

7. Revelation 7:14.

8. Jude 1.

blood from the wounds of the expiring Savior. Our eternal life is sure; because *He* lives, we shall live also. We shall behold the face of God with transport and delight, because *He* has gone up to prepare a place for us that where He is, we may be also. The Father has studiously linked every gospel privilege and every boon of the new covenant with the person of Jesus Christ, that in blessing you, He might at the same time honor His own dear Son. "Thus shall it be done to the man whom the king delighteth to honour;"[9] He shall be the King's almoner[10] to the poor and needy; He shall be the golden pipe through which streams of mercy shall flow to all His saints; His head shall be anointed with the holy oil which shall afterward bedew[11] the very skirts of His garments with the richest drops of perfume.

---

9. Esther 6:6.

10. An *almoner* was a court official who distributed alms to the poor on behalf of the ruler.

11. *Bedew* means "to wet with or as with dew."

3

———◦◦◦———

Christin the Covenant[1]

Again, it was necessary that Christ should be in the covenant because *there are many things there that would be nought without Him*. Our great redemption is in the covenant, but we have no redemption except through *His* blood. It is true that my righteousness is in the covenant, but I can have no righteousness apart from that which Christ has accomplished and which is imputed to me by God. It is very true that my eternal perfection is in the covenant, but the elect are only perfect in Christ. They are not perfect in themselves, nor will they ever be, until they have been washed and sanctified and perfected by the Holy Ghost. And even in heaven their perfection consists not so much in their sanctification as in their justification in Christ.

> Their beauty this, their glorious dress,
> Jesus the Lord their righteousness.[2]

In fact, if you take Christ out of the covenant, you have just done the same as if you should break the

---

1. From "Christ in the Covenant," *Spurgeon's Sermons* (1883; repr., Grand Rapids: Baker, 1983), 2:404–6. A sermon from Isaiah 59:8.

2. The text is from the hymn "Jesus, Thy Blood and Righteousness" (1739), by Nicolaus Ludwig, Graf von Zinzendorf, trans. John Wesley, in the public domain.

string of a necklace: all the jewels or beads or corals drop off and separate from each other. Christ is the golden string whereon the mercies of the covenant are threaded, and when you lay hold of Him, you have obtained the whole string of pearls. But if Christ is taken out, true there will be the pearls, but we cannot wear them, we cannot grasp them; they are separated, and poor faith can never know how to get hold of them. Oh! It is a mercy worth worlds that Christ is in the covenant.

4

Union with Christ[1]

Jesus is one with His elect federally. As in Adam, every
heir of flesh and blood has a personal interest
because Adam is the covenant head and representative of the race as considered under the law of works;
so under the law of grace, every redeemed soul is one
with the Lord from heaven, since He is the second
Adam, the sponsor and substitute of the elect in the
new covenant of love. The apostle Paul declares that
Levi was in the loins of Abraham when Melchize-
dek met him; it is a certain truth that the believer
was in the loins of Jesus Christ, the mediator, when
in old eternity the covenant settlements of grace
were decreed, ratified, and made sure forever. Thus,
whatever Christ has done, he has accomplished for
the whole body of His church. We were crucified in
Him and buried with Him (see Col. 2:10–13), and to
make it still more wonderful, we are risen with Him
and have even ascended with Him to the seats on
high.[2] It is thus that the church has fulfilled the law
and is "accepted in *the beloved.*"[3] It is thus that she is
regarded with complacency by the just Jehovah, for

---

1. From "Bands of Love: or, Union to Christ," *ST* (September
1865): 374–77.
2. Ephesians 2:6.
3. Ephesians 1:6, emphasis added.

He views her in Jesus and does not look upon her as separate from her covenant head. As the anointed redeemer of Israel, Christ Jesus has nothing distinct from His church, but all that He has He holds for her. Adam's righteousness was ours as long as he maintained it, and his sin was ours the moment that he committed it. In the same manner, all that the second Adam is or does is ours as well as His, seeing that He is our representative. Here is the foundation of the covenant of grace. This gracious system of representation and substitution, which moved Justin Martyr to cry out, "O blessed change, O sweet permutation!"[4] This, I say, is the very groundwork of the gospel of our salvation and is to be received with strong faith and rapturous joy. In every place the saints are perfectly one with Jesus.

---

4. Justin Martyr, *The Epistle of Mathetes to Diognetus*, chapter 9, in John Owen, *Meditations and Discourses on the Glory of Christ* (London: A.M. and R.R., 1684), 140.

5

⮕ ❖ ⬅

Christ's Sheep Will Never Perish[1]

*And I give unto them eternal life,
and they shall never perish.*
—John 10:28

The Christian should never think or speak lightly of unbelief. For a child of God to mistrust His love, His truth, His faithfulness, must be greatly displeasing to Him. How can we ever grieve Him by doubting His upholding grace? Christian! It is contrary to every promise of God's precious Word that you should ever be forgotten or left to perish. If it could be so, how could He be true who has said, "Can a woman forget her sucking child, that she should not have compassion on the son of her womb? yea, they may forget, yet will I not forget thee."[2] What of the value of that promise—"The mountains shall depart, and the hills be removed; but my kindness shall not depart from thee, neither shall the covenant of my peace be removed, saith the LORD that hath mercy on thee."[3] What of the truth of Christ's words—"I give

---

1. From "June 16," *Morning by Morning* (Nashville: Thomas Nelson, 2000), 156–57.

2. Isaiah 49:15.

3. Isaiah 54:10.

unto them eternal life; and they shall never perish, neither shall any man pluck them out of my hand. My Father, which gave them me, is greater than all; and no man is able to pluck them out of my Father's hand."[4] What of the doctrines of grace? They would be all disproved if one child of God should perish. What of the veracity of God, His honor, His power, His grace, His covenant, His oath, if any of those for whom Christ has died and who have put their trust in Him should nevertheless be cast away? Banish those unbelieving fears that so dishonor God. Arise, shake yourself from the dust, and put on your beautiful garments. Remember it is sinful to doubt His Word wherein He has promised you that you shall never perish. Let the eternal life within you express itself in confident rejoicing.

---

4. John 10:28–29.

6

Christ Died for Our Sins[1]

"Well," you say, "but Jesus Christ died as an exhibition of divine love." This is true in a certain sense, but from another point of view, of all the things I have ever heard, this does seem to me to be the most monstrous statement that could be made. That Jesus Christ, dying because of our sins, is a wonderful example of divine love, I do know, admit, and glory in. But that Christ's dying was an instance of divine love if He did not die because He bore our sins, I entirely deny. There is no exhibition of divine love in the death of Christ if it be not for our sins, but is an exhibition of a very different sort. The death of the perfect Son of God, per se, without its great object, does not exhibit love, but the reverse. What? Did God put to death His only begotten Son, the perfectly pure and holy being? Is this the *finale* of a life of obedience? Well, then, I see no love in God at all. It seems to me to be the reverse of love that it should be so. Apart from sin-bearing, the statement

---

1. From "Christ's Connection with Sinners the Source of His Glory," *Metropolitan Tabernacle Pulpit: Sermons Preached and Revised* (Pasadena, Tex.: Pilgrim Publications, 1988), 35:92–93. A sermon from Isaiah 53:12, delivered at the Metropolitan Tabernacle on February 17, 1889. All subsequent references to *Metropolitan Tabernacle Pulpit* are abbreviated *MTP*.

that Jesus needs to die the death of the cross to show us that His Father is full of love is sheer nonsense, but if He died in our room and stead, then the gift of Jesus Christ by the Father is undoubtedly a glorious instance of divine love. Behold and wonder that "God so loved the world, that he gave his only begotten Son, that whosoever believes in him should not perish, but have everlasting life."[2] This is love, if you please, but not the mere fact that the Son of God should be put to death. That were a thing altogether unaccountable, not to be justified, but to be looked upon as a horrible mystery never to be explained— that the blessed Son of God should die—if we did not receive this full and complete explanation, "He bare the sin of many."[3]

If our Lord's bearing our sin for us is not the gospel, I have no gospel to preach. Brethren, I have fooled you these five-and-thirty years if this is not the gospel. I am a lost man if this is not the gospel, for I have no hope beneath the copes[4] of heaven, neither in time nor in eternity, save only in this belief that Jesus, in my stead, bore both my punishment and sin.

If our Lord did so bear our sin, we have a firm and joyous confidence. God would not accept a substitute in our place and then punish *us*. If Jesus suffered in my stead, I shall not suffer. If another has gone to prison and to death for me, I shall not go there. If the axe has fallen on the neck of Him that took my place, justice is satisfied and the law

---

2. John 3:16.

3. Isaiah 53:12.

4. A *cope* was a priestly vestment or robe.

is vindicated; I am free, happy, joyful, grateful, and therefore bound forever to serve Him who loved me and gave Himself for me. I do not know how you look upon this doctrine, but it seems to me to be something worth telling everywhere. I would like to make every wind bear it on its wings and every wave waft it on its crest. There is a just and righteous way to forgive sin, by Jesus bearing the death penalty in the sinners' stead, that whosoever believes in Him should be justified from all things, from which the Law could not deliver him.

Sons at 21 Years Old

C. H. Spurgeon, *C. H. Spurgeon's Autobiography. Compiled from His Diary, Letters, and Records.* Vol. 3. 4 vols (London: Passmore and Alabaster, 1899), 292.

7

No Atonement, No Gospel[1]

Dear Friends,

With great pleasure I have prepared this sermon upon that truth which lies at the heart of the Christian faith. The denial of the substitutionary sacrifice of our Lord is the abjuration of Christianity. Without atonement by the death of the Savior, there is no gospel. I do not conceive "substitution" to be an explanation of atonement but to be the very essence of it. Those of us who have receive the Lord Jesus as our expiation and righteousness know what divine power dwells in that precious truth.

In a few days I hope to be on my way home; indeed, I may be so when this sermon is published. I crave a kind remembrance in the prayers of the faithful. May there be years of useful preaching and fruitful hearing in store for preachers and readers!

Yours, in Christ Jesus,

C. H. Spurgeon
Mentone, Feb. 11, 1889

---

1. From "Letter from Mr. Spurgeon [to his congregation from Mentone]," *MTP*, 35:96.

8

The Necessity of Atonement[1]

Besides that, beloved, *that sin should not be pardoned without an atonement is for the welfare of the universe.* This world is but a speck compared with the universe of God. We cannot even imagine the multitudes of beings over which the great Lawgiver has rule, and if it could be whispered anywhere in that universe that on this planet God tampered with the law, set aside justice, or did anything, in fact, to save His own chosen so that He threw His own threats behind His back and disregarded His own solemn ordinance, why, this report would strike at the foundations of the eternal throng! Is God unjust in any case? Then how could He judge the universe? What creatures, then, would fear God, when they knew that He could play fast and loose with justice? It would be a calamity even greater than hell itself that sin should go unpunished. The very reins of moral order would be snatched from the hand of the great Charioteer, and I know not what mischief would happen. Evil would then have mounted to the high throne of God and would have become supreme throughout His domains. It is for the welfare of the universe, throughout the ages,

---

1. From "Redemption through Blood, the Gracious Forgiveness of Sins," *MTP*, 37:305–6. A sermon from Ephesians 1:7 delivered at the Metropolitan Tabernacle on June 7, 1891.

that in the forgiveness of sins there should be redemption by blood. Let lovers of anarchy cavil[2] at it, but let good men accept the sacrifice of the Son of God with joy as the great establishment of law and justice.

Moreover, *this also is arranged for our comfort and assurance of heart.* I protest before you all that if I had been anywhere assured, when I was under conviction of sin, that God could forgive me outright without any atonement, it would have yielded no sort of satisfaction to me, for my conscience was sitting in judgment upon myself, and I felt that if I were on the throne of God, I must condemn myself to hell. Even if I could have derived a temporary comfort from the notion of forgiveness apart from atonement, the question would afterward have come up—how is this just? If God does not punish me, He ought to do so; how can He do otherwise? He must be just, or He is not God. It must be that such sin as mine should bring punishment upon itself. Never, until I understood the great truth of the substitutionary death of Christ, could my conscience get a moment's peace. If an atonement was not necessary for God, it certainly was necessary for me, and it seems to me necessary to every conscience that is fairly instructed as to the absolute certainty that sin involves deserved sorrow and that every transgression and every iniquity must have its just recompense of reward. It was necessary for the perpetual peace of every enlightened conscience that the glorious atonement should have been provided.

---

2. *Cavil* means "to make a petty or unnecessary objection."

9

Substitution[1]

I have always considered, with Luther and Calvin, that the sum and substance of the gospel lies in the word *substitution*—Christ standing in the stead of man. If I understand the gospel, it is this: I deserve to be lost forever; the only reason why I should not be damned is that Christ was punished in my stead, and there is no need to execute a sentence twice for sin. On the other hand, I know I cannot enter heaven unless I have a perfect righteousness; I am absolutely certain I shall never have one of my own for I find I sin every day, but then Christ has a perfect righteousness, and He said: "There, poor sinner, take My garment and put it on; you should stand before God as if you were Christ, and I will stand before God as if I had been the sinner; I will suffer in the sinner's stead, and you shall be rewarded for works that you did not do but that I did for you." I find it very convenient every day to come to Christ as a sinner as I came at first. "You are no saint," says the devil. Well, if I am not, I am a sinner, and Jesus Christ came into the world to save sinners. Sink or swim, I go to Him; of other hope, I have none. By looking to

1. From C. H. Spurgeon, *The Autobiography of Charles H. Spurgeon* (Nashville: Publishing House of the Methodist Episcopal Church South, 1900), 1:113.

Him, I received all the faith which inspired me with confidence in His grace, and the word that first drew my soul—"Look unto me"[2]—still rings its clarion note in my ears. There I once found conversion, and there I shall forever find refreshment and renewal.

---

2. Isaiah 45:22.

10

━━━ ◄●► ━━━

The Scapegoat[1]

The first goat was a type of the atonement[2]; the second is the type of the effect of the atonement.[3] The second goat went away after the first was slaughtered, carrying the sins of the people on its head, and so it sets forth, as a scapegoat, how our sins are carried away into the depth of the wilderness. There was this year exhibited in the Art Union[4] a fine picture of the scapegoat dying in the wilderness: it was represented with a burning sky above it, its feet sticking in the mire, surrounded by hundreds of skeletons, and there dying a doleful[5] and miserable death. Now, that was just a piece of gratuitous nonsense, for there is nothing in the Scripture that warrants it in the least degree. The rabbis tell us that this goat was taken by a man into the wilderness and

---

1. From "The Day of Atonement," *NPSP*, 2:334–35. A sermon from Leviticus 16:34 delivered at New Park Street Chapel, Southwark, on August 10, 1856.

2. Leviticus 16:15.

3. Leviticus 16:20.

4. The Art Union of London, which from 1837 to 1912 was an organization that distributed works of art among its subscribers by lottery. Like other similar organizations, the Art Union of London was a means of promoting contemporary art and cultivating patrons of the arts.

5. *Doleful* means "cheerless."

there tumbled down a high rock to die, but, as an excellent commentator says, if the man did push it down the rock, he did more than God ever told him to do. God told him to take a goat and let it go; as to what became of it, neither you nor I know anything because that is purposely left out. Our Lord Jesus Christ has taken away our sins upon His head, just as the scapegoat, and He is gone from us—that is all; the goat was not a type in its dying or in regard to its subsequent fate. God has only told us that it should be taken by the hand of a fit man into the wilderness. The most correct account seems to be that of one Rabbi Jarchi,[6] who says that they generally took the goat twelve miles out of Jerusalem, and at each mile there was a booth provided where the man who took it might refresh himself till he came to the tenth mile, when there was no more rest for him till he had seen the goat go. When he had come to the last mile, he stood and looked at the goat till it was gone and he could see it no more. Then the people's sins were all gone too. Now, what a fine type that is if you do not inquire any further! But it you will get meddling where God intended you to be in ignorance, you will get nothing by it.

This scapegoat was not designed to show us the victim or the sacrifice but simply what became of the sins. The sins of the people are confessed upon that head: the goat is going; the people lose sight of it; a fit man goes with it; the sins are going from them, and

---

6. This is an archaic name for Shlomo Yitzchaki, now more commonly known as Rashi, who was a medieval French rabbi and popular commenter on Talmud and the Tanakh.

now the man has arrived at his destination; the man sees the goat in the distance skipping here and there over the mountains, glad of its liberty; it is not quite gone; a little farther, and now it is lost to sight. The man returns and says he can no longer see it; then the people clap their hands, for their sins are all gone too. Oh! Soul, can you see your sins all gone? We may have to take a long journey and carry our sins with us, but oh! How we watch and watch till they are utterly cast into the wilderness of forgetfulness where they shall never be found anymore against us forever. But mark, this goat did not sacrificially make the atonement; it was a type of the sins going away, and so it was a type of the atonement. For you know, since our sins are thereby lost, it is the fruit of the atonement, but the sacrifice is the means of making it.

So we have this great and glorious thought before us, that by the death of Christ there was full, free, perfect remission for all those whose sins are laid upon His head. For I would have you notice that on this day all sins were laid on the scapegoat's head—sins of presumption, sins of ignorance, sins of uncleanness, sins little and sins great, sins few and sins many, sins against the law, sins against morality, sins against ceremonies, sins of all kinds were taken away on that great day of atonement. Sinner, oh, that you had a share in my Master's atonement! Oh! That you could see Him slaughtered on the cross! Then you might see Him go away, leading captivity captive and taking your sins where they might never be found.

━━━━ ━◦(◦)◦━ ━━━━

11

Atonement and Jubilee[1]

Turn to Leviticus 25:9, and you will read: "Then shalt thou cause the trumpet of the jubilee to sound on the tenth day of the seventh month, in the day of atonement shall ye make the trumpet sound throughout all your land." So that one of the effects of the atonement was set forth to us in the fact that when the year of jubilee came, it was not on the first day of the year that it was proclaimed, but "on the tenth day of the seventh month" Ay, methinks that was the best part of it. The scapegoat is gone, and the sins are gone, and no sooner are they gone than the silver trumpet sounds,

> The year of jubilee is come,
> Return ye ransomed sinners, home.[2]

On that day sinners go free; on that day our poor mortgaged lands are liberated and our poor estates, which have been forfeited by our spiritual bankruptcy, are all returned to us. So when Jesus dies, slaves win their liberty and lost ones receive spiritual life again; when He dies, heaven, the long-lost

---

1. From "The Day of Atonement," in *NPSP*, 2:335.

2. From the hymn "Blow Ye the Trumpet, Blow" (1750), by Charles Wesley, in the public domain.

inheritance, is ours. Blessed day! Atonement and jubilee ought to go together. Have you ever had a jubilee, my friends, in your hearts? If you have not, I can tell you it is because you have not had a day of atonement.

12

Christ, Our Scapegoat[1]

Now, how am I to get rid of this sin that is in me, as to the evil consequences inherent within the evil? Suppose God to be perfectly reconciled to me so far, yet still there is an evil that mischief brings upon me in itself, apart from God, and how do I get rid of that? Why, through the scapegoat.

The sin of the people was, first of all, transferred to this scapegoat—all confessed and all laid on the scapegoat. Then by divine appointment, the scapegoat being chosen by lot and the lot being guided by God, it was accepted as being the substitute for the people. The scapegoat was then taken away, and what was done with it? Why, nothing was done with it, but this—it was relinquished—it was given up. Now, can I get out what I mean? I am very much afraid I cannot. Our Lord Jesus Christ took upon Himself the sin of His people, and He was given up to evil, that is to say, to all the power that evil could put out against Him—first in the wilderness, tempted from all quarters, tempted by the temptations of Satan, and then in the garden, tempted in such a way as you

1. From "The Day of Atonement," *MTP*, 60:162–63. A sermon from Leviticus 16:34 delivered at the Metropolitan Tabernacle on May 9, 1869.

and I never were—the powers of evil were let loose upon Him as they never were upon us.

Did He not say, "This is your hour, and the power of darkness"?[2] And so dreadful was the assault of evil upon Him, the devil going forth as the type and incarnation of evil, that He sweated, as it were, great drops of blood falling to the ground while especially on the tree, where the conflict reached its climax, and He was given up.

That cry, "My God, My God, why hast thou forsaken me?"[3] is like the cry of the goat when it is given up, quite given up, and led away. Evil was permitted to work out in Him all its own dread hatefulness and havoc, to which it must bring to our spirits unless God interposed to stop evil from making the soul become unutterably wretched, even unto death.

I do not know how to get out the thought which seems to be in my soul, but I do rejoice to think that all the evil I have ever done shall not go on to plague and vex me because it has vexed and plagued Him— that all the essential misery that lies in my past sin, which must, even if God forgave it, still come back to sting and torment me throughout all my existence, was so laid on Him and so spent all its force and venom on Him, who was given up to it, that it will never touch me again.

You know, brethren, there was no other man who could have borne all that power of evil but our Lord. It all fell on Him, and yet it never stained His matchless purity and perfection of character. The

---

2. Luke 22:53.
3. Psalm 22:1; Matthew 27:46.

misery of it came to Him, but the guilt of it could never defile Him. The misery of sin spent itself on the lonely One who was given up to its awful force, but it could do no more. The type says nothing about the scapegoat, whether it died or not, and Christ did not die because of the misery of His spirit; He died for quite another reason and in another sense, laying down His life for His people.

There is something, I think, interesting in this if we can carry it out, but there is this to be said—by that scapegoat being thus given up, the sin of the congregation was taken away, all taken away, and all gone. And so, through Jesus Christ having borne our sicknesses and carried our sorrows, the whole force and power of evil to do damning mischief against a saint has been taken away forever from every one of us who have laid our hands by faith upon His dear and blessed head. It is gone; the sin is gone, gone into the wilderness, where it shall never be found against us anymore forever.

Pastor's College Library

C. H. Spurgeon, *C. H. Spurgeon's Autobiography. Compiled from His Diary, Letters, and Records.* Vol. 3. 4 vols (London: Passmore and Alabaster, 1899), 355.

13

Healed by His Stripes[1]

The stripes of Jesus do heal men; they have healed many of us. It does not look as if it could effect so great a cure, but the fact is undeniable. I often hear people say, "If you preach this faith in Jesus Christ as saving men, they will be careless about holy living." I am as good a witness on that point as anybody, for I live every day in the midst of men who are trusting to the stripes of Jesus for their salvation, and I have seen no ill effect follow from such trust, but I have seen the very reverse. I bear testimony that I have seen the very worst of men become the very best of men by believing in the Lord Jesus Christ. These stripes heal in a surprising manner the moral diseases of those who seemed past remedy.

The character is healed. I have seen the drunkard become sober, the harlot become chaste, the passionate man become gentle, the covetous man become liberal, and the liar become truthful, simply by trusting in the sufferings of Jesus. If it did not make good men of them, it would not really do anything for

1. From "Healing by the Stripes of Jesus," in C. H. Spurgeon, *Messages to the Multitude: Being Ten Representative Sermons* (London: Sampson Low, Marston & Company, 1892), 222–25. A sermon from Isaiah 53:5 that was intended for reading at the Metropolitan Tabernacle on January 1, 1888.

them, for you must judge men by their fruits, after all, and if the fruits are not changed, the tree is not changed. Character is everything: if the character is not set right, the man is not saved. But we say it without fear of contradiction that the atoning sacrifice, applied to the heart, heals the disease of sin. If you doubt it, try it. He that believes in Jesus is sanctified as well as justified; by faith he becomes henceforth an altogether changed man.

The conscience is healed of its smart.[2] Sin crushed the man's soul; he was spiritless and joyless, but the moment he believed in Jesus, he leaped into light. Often you can see a change in the very look of the man's face; the cloud flies from the countenance when guilt goes from the conscience. Scores of times, when I have been talking with those bowed down with sin's burden, they have looked as though they were qualifying for an asylum through inward grief, but when they have caught the thought, "Christ stood for me, and if I trust in Him, I have the sign that He did so and I am clear," their faces have been lit up as with a glimpse of heaven.

Gratitude for such great mercy causes a change of thought toward God, and so *it heals the judgment*, and by this means the affections are turned in the right way, and *the heart is healed*. Sin is no longer loved, but God is loved, and holiness is desired. *The whole man is healed*, and the whole life is changed. Many of you know how light of heart faith in Jesus makes you, how the troubles of life lose their weight and the fear of death ceases to cause bondage. You rejoice in the

---

2. *Smart* in this context means "grief or remorse."

Lord, for the blessed remedy of the stripes of Jesus is applied to your soul by faith in Him.

The fact that "with his stripes we are healed"[3] is a matter in evidence. I shall take liberty to bear my own witness. If it were necessary, I could call thousands of persons, my daily acquaintances, who can say that with the stripes of Jesus they are healed, but I must not therefore withhold my personal testimony. If I had suffered from a dreadful disease, and a physician had given me a remedy that had healed me, I should not be ashamed to tell you all about it, but I would quote my own case as an argument with you to try my physician. Years ago, when I was a youth, the burden of my sin was exceedingly heavy upon me. I had fallen into no gross vices and should not have been regarded by any one as being especially a transgressor, but I regarded myself as such, and I had good reason for so doing. My conscience was sensitive because it was enlightened, and I judged that, having had a godly father and a praying mother and having been trained in the ways of piety, I had sinned against much light, and consequently there was a greater degree of guilt in my sin than in that of others who were my youthful associates but had not enjoyed my advantages. I could not enjoy the sports of youth because I felt that I had done violence to my conscience. I would seek my chamber and there sit alone, read my Bible, and pray for forgiveness, but peace did not come to me. Books such as Baxter's *Call to the Unconverted* and Doddridge's *Rise*

---

3. Isaiah 53:5.

and Progress I read over and over again.[4] Early in the morning I would awake and read the most earnest religious books I could find, desiring to be eased of my burden of sin. I was not always thus dull, but at times my misery of soul was very great. The words of the weeping prophet and of Job were such as suited my mournful case. I would have chosen death rather than life. I tried to do as well as I could and to behave myself aright, but in my own judgment I grew worse and worse. I felt more and more despondent. I attended every place of worship within my reach, but I heard nothing which gave me lasting comfort till one day I heard a simple preacher of the gospel speak from the text, "Look unto Me, and be ye saved, all the ends of the earth."[5] When he told me that all I had to do was to "look" to Jesus—to Jesus the crucified One—I could scarcely believe it. He went on and said, "Look, look, look!" He added, "There is a young man, under the left-hand gallery there, who is very miserable; he will have no peace until he looks to Jesus." And then he cried, "Look! Look! Young man, look!" I did look, and in that moment relief came to me, and I felt such overflowing joy that I could have stood up and cried, "Hallelujah! Glory be to God, I am delivered from the burden of my sin!"

---

4. These two books are Richard Baxter, *A Call to the Unconverted to Turn and Live* (1657) and Philip Doddridge, *The Rise and Progress of Religion in the Soul* (1761). The former is one of the key Puritan evangelistic booklets, while the latter, though longer, served a similar purpose a century later among later evangelicals, especially in the Church of England. Both works were perennially reprinted throughout the nineteenth century.

5. Isaiah 45:22

14

Forgiveness[1]

There is no sinner out of hell so black that God cannot wash him white. There is not out of the pit one so guilty that God is not able and willing to forgive him, for He declares the wondrous fact—"I, even I, am he that blots out thy transgressions."[2]

Notice once more, that it is a present forgiveness. It does not say, "I am He who will blot out your transgressions," but suggests that He blots them out now. There are some who believe, or at least seem to imagine, that it is not possible to know whether our sins are forgiven in this life. We may have hope, it is thought, that at last there will be a balance to strike on our side. But this will not satisfy the poor soul who is really seeking pardon and is anxious to find it, and God has therefore blessedly told us that He blots out our sin now, that He will do it at any moment the sinner believes. As soon as he trusts in his crucified God, all his sins are forgiven, whether past, present, or to come. Even supposing that he is yet to commit them, they are all pardoned. If I live eighty years after I receive pardon, doubtless I shall fall into many errors, but the one pardon will avail

---

1. From "Forgiveness," *NPSP*, 1:186. A sermon on Isaiah 43:25 delivered at Exeter Hall on May 20, 1855.

2. Isaiah 43:25.

for them as well as for the past. Jesus Christ bore our punishment, and God will never require at my hands the fulfillment of that law which Christ has honored in my stead, for then there would be injustice in heaven and that would be far from God. It is no more possible for a pardoned man to be lost than for Christ to be lost, because Christ is the sinner's surety. Jehovah will never require my debt to be paid twice. Let none impute injustice to the God of the whole earth; let none suppose that He will twice exact the penalty of one sin. If you have been the chief of sinners, you may have the chief of sinner's forgiveness, and God can bestow it now.

I cannot help but notice the completeness of this forgiveness. Suppose you call on your creditor and say to him, "I have nothing to pay with." "Well," says he, "I can issue a distress[3] against you and place you in prison and keep you there." You still reply that you have nothing and he must do what he can. Suppose he should then say, "I will forgive all." You now stand amazed and say, "Can it be possible that you will give me that great debt of a thousand pounds?" He replies, "Yes, I will." You ask, "But how am I to know it?"

There is a bond: he takes it and crosses it all out and hands it back to you and says, "There is a full discharge; I have blotted it all out." So does the Lord deal with penitents. He has a book in which all your debts are written, but with the blood of Christ He crosses out the handwriting of ordinances that is there written against you. The bond is destroyed, and

---

3. A *distress* was a claim for a debt that involved the seizure of goods.

he will not demand payment for it again. The devil will sometimes insinuate to the contrary, as he did to Martin Luther.[4] "Bring me the catalogue of my sins," said Luther, and the devil brought a scroll black and long. "Is that all?" said Luther. "No," said the devil, and he brought yet another. "And now," said the heroic saint of God, "write at the foot of the scroll: 'The blood of Jesus Christ his Son cleanseth us from all sin.'"[5] That is a full discharge.

---

4. Spurgeon is referencing a common story about Martin Luther that has been recounted by many of his biographers, though the exact wording varies from source to source. For example, see Roland H. Bainton, *Here I Stand: A Life of Martin Luther* (New York: Merdian, 1995), 284.

5. 1 John 1:7.

15

Crucified with Christ[1]

I am crucified with Christ.
—Galatians 2:20

The Lord Jesus Christ acted in what He did as a great public representative person, and His dying upon the cross was the virtual dying of all His people. Then all His saints rendered unto justice what was due and made an expiation to divine vengeance for all their sins. The apostle of the gentiles delighted to think that as one of Christ's chosen people, he died upon the cross in Christ. He did more than believe this doctrinally, he accepted it confidently, resting his hope upon it. He believed that by virtue of Christ's death, he had satisfied divine justice and found reconciliation with God. Beloved, what a blessed thing it is when the soul can, as it were, stretch itself upon the cross of Christ and say, "I am dead; the law has slain me, and I am therefore free from its power, because in my Surety I have borne the curse, and in the Person of my substitute the whole that the law could do by way of condemnation has been executed upon me, for I am crucified with Christ."

1. From "December 14," *Evening by Evening* (Nashville: Thomas Nelson, 2000), 320–21.

But Paul meant even more than this. He not only believed in Christ's death and trusted in it, but he actually felt its power in himself in causing the crucifixion of his old corrupt nature. When he saw the pleasures of sin, he said, "I cannot enjoy these: I am dead to them." Such is the experience of every true Christian. Having received Christ, he is to this world as one who is utterly dead. Yet, while conscious of death to the world, he can, at the same time, exclaim with the apostle, "Nevertheless I live." He is fully alive unto God. The Christian's life is a matchless riddle. No worldling[2] can comprehend it; even the believer himself cannot understand it. Dead, yet alive! Crucified with Christ, and yet at the same time risen with Christ in newness of life! Union with the suffering, bleeding Savior and death to the world and sin are soul-cheering things. O for more enjoyment of them!

---

2. *Worldling* is an archaic term that means "an unbeliever"—that is, one who is of the world rather than of God.

16

All Hail King Jesus[1]

The LORD is King for ever and ever.
—Psalm 10:16

Jesus Christ is no despotic claimant of divine right, but He is really and truly the Lord's anointed! "It pleased the Father that in him should all fulness dwell."[2] God has given to Him all power and all authority. As the Son of man, He is now head over all things to His church, and He reigns over heaven and earth and hell with the keys of life and death at His girdle. Certain princes have delighted to call themselves kings by the popular will, and certainly our Lord Jesus Christ is such in His church. If it could be put to the vote whether He should be king in the church, every believing heart would crown Him. O that we could crown Him more gloriously than we do! We would count no expense to be wasted that could glorify Christ. Suffering would be pleasure and loss would be gain, if thereby we could surround His brow with brighter crowns and make Him more glorious in the eyes of men and angels.

Yes, He shall reign. Long live the King! All hail to thee, King Jesus! Go forth, you virgin souls who love

---

1. From "April 27," *Evening by Evening*, 108–9.
2. Colossians 1:19.

your Lord; bow at His feet, strew His way with the lilies of your love and the roses of your gratitude: "Bring forth the royal diadem, and crown him Lord of all."[3] Moreover, our Lord Jesus is king in Zion by right of conquest: He has taken and carried by storm the hearts of His people and has slain their enemies who held them in cruel bondage. In the Red Sea of His own blood, our Redeemer has drowned the pharaoh of our sins? Shall He not be king in Jeshurun?[4] He has delivered us from the iron yoke and heavy curse of the law. Shall not the Liberator be crowned? We are His portion, whom He has taken out of the hand of the Amorite with His sword and with His bow. Who shall snatch His conquest from His hand? All hail, King Jesus! We gladly own your gentle sway[5]! Rule in our hearts forever, you lovely Prince of Peace.

---

3. From the first stanza of Edward Perronet, "All Hail the Power of Jesus' Name" (1779), in the public domain.

4. Jeshurun was a poetic name used for Israel in Deuteronomy 32:15; 33:5, 26; Isaiah 44:2.

5. In context, *sway* means "sovereign rule or power."

17

The Lord's Supper as a
Picture of Redemption[1]

I suppose there would be a reference [when discussing the Lord's Supper] to the great redemption out of Egypt. Every Israelite ought to have had confidence in God after what He had done for the people in redeeming them out of Egypt. To every one of the seed of Jacob, it was a grand argument to enforce the precept, "Fear not."[2]

But I take it that the chief reference of these words is to that redemption that has been accomplished for us by Him who loved us and washed us from our sins in His own blood. Let us think of it for a minute or two before we break the bread and drink of the cup.

The remembrance of this transcendent redemption ought to comfort us in all times of *perplexity*. When we cannot see our way or cannot make out what to do, we need not be at all troubled concerning it, for the Lord Jehovah can see a way out of every intricacy. In the glorious sacrifice of Jesus, we see the justice of God magnified, for He laid sin on the blessed Lord, who had become one with His chosen. Jesus identified Himself with His people, and therefore

---

1. From "A Talk with a Few Friends at the Lord's Table," *ST* (March 1888): 106–7.

2. This is an allusion to Isaiah 43:1. The latter part of the verse is cited below.

their sin was soon laid upon Him, and the sword of the Lord awoke against Him. He was not taken arbitrarily to be a victim, but He was a voluntary sufferer because His relationship amounted to covenant oneness with them and it behooved Christ to suffer.[3] Herein is a wisdom which must be more than equal to all minor perplexities. Hear this, then, O poor soul in suspense! The Lord says, "I have redeemed thee."[4] Furthermore, "I have already brought thee out of the labyrinth in which you were lost by sin, and therefore I will take you out of the meshes of the net of temptation, and lead you through the maze of trial. I will bring the blind by a way that they know not and lead them in paths which they have not known. I will bring again from Bashan,[5] I will bring up my people from the depths of the sea." Let us commit our way unto the Lord. Mine is a peculiarly difficult one, but I know that my Redeemer lives, and He will lead me by a right way. He will be our guide even unto death, and after death He will guide us through those unknown tracks of the mysterious region and cause us to rest with Him forever.

---

3. This is an allusion to Luke 24:46.

4. Isaiah 43:1.

5. Bashan was part of the Promised Land that is frequently mentioned in the Old Testament. Bashan coincides with present-day Golan Heights in Palestine.

18

A Full Christ[1]

If I search you through and through, even with a candle, there is not a good thing, nor a rag of a good thing, to be found in you. But what then? This only proves what an empty sinner you are, and there is a full Christ for all empty sinners. Only let them be but empty, and the Master is ready enough to fill them. Confess your emptiness, acknowledge that in you dwells no good thing and ask Him, according to the infinitude of His mercy, the multitude of His tender mercies, to fill you, even now. I am sure that the moment when we are accepted in Christ is the moment when we realize our need of Christ and yield up our emptiness to be filled from His fullness. We generally get Christ, I think, when we acknowledge ourselves to be the very lowest and most unworthy of men. He that is bankrupt and beggared of all consciousness of creature merit and of all human hope is the man to whom the riches of the covenant of grace most surely belong.

I beg you to think much of the fullness of Christ. You are full of sin; well, but He is full of mercy. You are full of guilt; He is full of atoning merit. You are

1. From "A Full Christ for Empty Sinners and Saints," *ST* (June 1893): 254–55.

full of hardness of heart; He is full of long-suffering and tenderness toward you. You are full of mistakes; He is full of wisdom. You are empty of all power; He is full of might. Though you have nothing, He has everything. The mercy is that just in those very points where you fail, Christ excels, and His merits just fit your demerits as the key fits the lock. Christ was prepared on purpose for such a one as you are! His character and His work precisely meet the needs of your sad and fallen condition.

Now, second, I want to say a word or two about a *full Christ for empty saints*. I do not think we know much about Christ yet; at any rate, we are but beginners in the things of God. Some of our elder brethren may know more, but I think I know enough to say that probably he who knows most of Christ has discovered most of his own emptiness, that in proportion as we go down, Christ goes up, and as we see more and more of the deep depravity of our own hearts, we shall see more and more of the amazing excellence of the person and work of our Lord Jesus Christ.

19

Seeing the Cross[1]

Paul says that Christ was visibly set forth as crucified among them.[2] Did you ever see Christ in this way? I do not ask whether you ever saw a vision. Who wishes for that? I do not ask whether your imagination was so worked upon that you thought you saw the Savior. There would be no particular use in that, for thousands did actually see Him on the cross, and they thrust out their tongues at Him and perished in their sins. But let me tell you that it is one of the most strengthening things to our piety to get to feel by faith as though we did behold the Savior. We do not expect to *see* Him until He comes, yet, when we have been alone in our chamber, we have as much realized His presence without the use of our eyes as if we had literally seen Him. He has been certainly sensibly crucified before us, for this is the point. Paul says that he had set forth Christ with such vividness—he had word-painted so thoroughly well, he had spoken so plainly and so simply, that they seemed to say, "We see it: Christ in our stead, Christ bleeding for our sin." They seemed to see Him as if He were before them in their midst. My dear friends, do not say, "Christ

1. From "Men Bewitched," *MTP*, 26:389–90. A sermon from Galatians 3:1 delivered at the Metropolitan Tabernacle.

2. See Galatians 3:1.

died on Calvary. That is thousands of miles off." I
know that He did, but what matters where He died,
as to locality? He loved you and gave Himself for
you. Let Him be to you as though He were crucified
at Newington Butts[3] and as though His cross were
in the middle of this tabernacle. "Oh, but He died
nineteen hundred years ago." I know that He did, but
the efficacy of His death is a thing of today. "He died
unto sin once,"[4] and that once pours the splendor of
its efficacy all down the ages, and the thing for you
to do is to feel as if you saw Him dying *now*, on the
tree *now*—you standing immediately at the foot of
the cross and looking up and seeing Him looking
down from that cross and saying, "I did all this for
you." Can you not ask the Lord to make it as vivid
as that to you? I want, while I am looking upon this
great throng, to forget you all, and to see Jesus standing here with the nail prints. Oh, if I could see Him,
how humbly I would throw myself at His feet! With
what love would I embrace Him! With what reverence would I adore Him! But my Master, I am so sure
of the fact that Thou didst die in my stead and that
my sins were laid on Thee, that even now I see Thee
discharging all my debts and bearing all my curse.
Though Thou art gone to glory, yet I vividly realize
that Thou wast here. This has become a fact to me.

---

3. Newington Butts Theatre is famous for possibly being the earli-
est theater in London.

4. Romans 6:10.

A. & G. Taylor, "N/A," n.d., photograph card, 4.125 x 2 in. Published by A. & G. Taylor, London. Held at The Spurgeon Library, Midwestern Baptist Theological Seminary, Kansas City, Missouri.

20

My Sole Hope for Heaven[1]

When I was anxious about the possibility of the just God pardoning me, I understood and saw by faith that He who is the Son of God had become man. In His own blessed person, He did this for my sin, which He bore in His own body on the tree. I saw that the chastisement of my peace was laid on Him and that with His stripes I was healed.[2] It was because the Son of God, supremely glorious in His matchless person, undertook to vindicate the law by bearing the sentence due to me, that therefore God was able to pass by my sin. My sole hope for heaven lies in the full atonement made on Calvary's cross for the ungodly. On that I firmly rely. I have not a shadow of hope anywhere else.

Personally, I could never have overcome my own sinfulness. I tried and failed. My evil propensities were too many for me, till, in the belief that Christ died for me, I cast my guilty soul on Him, and then I received a conquering principle by which I overcame my sinful self. The doctrine of the cross can be used to slay sin, even as the old warriors use their huge two-handed swords and mowed down their foes at

---

1. From *Autobiography*, 1:99.
2. This is an allusion to Isaiah 53:5.

every stroke. There is nothing like faith in the sinners' Friend: it overcomes all evil. If Christ has died for me, ungodly as I am, without strength as I am, then I cannot live in sin any longer but must arouse myself to love and serve Him who has redeemed me. I cannot trifle with the evil that slew my best Friend. I must be holy for His sake. How can I live in sin when He has died to save me from it?

21

The Comfort of Christ's Sacrifice[1]

Furthermore (as preachers say), is not the gospel calculated to make men happy when it is really understood, believed, and enjoyed? You believe that Jesus Christ is man in our nature, that the Word was made flesh. Did not this grand truth set all heaven ablaze with splendor on the night of the nativity, while angels chanted midnight chorales, and should it not also set your heart aglow with sacred joy every night and every day, while all your powers and passions sing with gratitude?

You believe that Jesus died for sinners. The doctrine of the atonement is earth's heaven-given light, by which the dark despair of humanity is chased away. Do you believe yourself to be forgiven and washed in the precious blood, and does your heart never say, "I will praise thee every day, now Thine anger's turned away"?[2]

Do you derive no comfort "from the bleeding sacrifice"?[3] Shall the praises of Jesus never be your pleasant song? It seems to me that if one had to

---

1. From "Bells for the Horses," *ST* (March 1866), 100–101. This article offers a reflection on Zechariah 14:20.

2. See Isaiah 12:1.

3. From the first stanza of Charles Wesley, "Arise, My Soul, Arise" (1742), in the public domain.

conceive beforehand, without observation, what state of mind that heart would be in which had thoroughly received the gospel of peace, one would be constrained to mention, together with other sacred effects, *happiness* as a most prominent result. Surely, I should say, a soul elect of God, bought with blood, called by the Spirit, made a partaker of heavenly banquets, and ordained unto eternal life, must have a new song put into its mouth. We have fellowship with a Savior whose joys were as deep, though not so apparent as His agonies, and we may find peace where He found His, namely, in contemplation of the glory that the Father receives in the work of His dear Son.

22

Mourning and Resting in the Cross[1]

Brethren, we cannot talk of the cross of Christ except in subdued tones. If you think you can laugh and sport yourself because your sin is forgiven, you know nothing of the matter. Sin has been pardoned at such a price that we cannot henceforth trifle with it. The sacrifice was so august[2] that we must ever speak of it with holy trembling. I always feel a suspicion of those converts who get up and glibly boast that once they were drunkards, thieves, blasphemers, and so forth. Brother, if you do tell the story of your sin, blush scarlet to think it should be true. I am ashamed to hear a man talk of his sins as an old Greenwich pensioner[3] might talk of his sea fights. I hate to hear a man exhibiting his old lusts as if they were scars of honor.

Friend, these things are disgraceful to you, however much the putting of them away may be to the honor and glory of God, and they are to be spoken

---

1. From "The Annual Atonement," *MTP*, 32:551–52. A sermon from Leviticus 16:30 delivered at the Metropolitan Tabernacle on October 3, 1886.

2. In this context, *august* means "impressive."

3. A Greenwich pensioner was a retired sailor or marine who lived in retirement in the Royal Hospital for Seamen in Greenwich. The institution was not for medical care but for hospitality because it provided room, board, and pension payments for its residents and their dependents.

of by you with shame and confusion of face. Afflict your soul when you remember what you once were.

On the day of atonement, they were to afflict their souls, and yet they were to rest. Can these things come together—mourning and resting? Oh yes, you and I know how they meet in one bosom. I never am so truly happy as when a sober sadness tinges my joy. When I am fullest of joy I could weep my life away at Jesus's feet. Nothing is really sweeter than the bitterness of repentance. Nothing is more healthy than self-abhorrence mixed with the grateful love which hides itself in the wounds of Jesus. The purified people were to rest; they were to rest from all servile work. I will never do a hand's turn to save myself by my own merits, works, or feelings. I am done forever with all interference with my Lord's sole work. Salvation as to its meritorious cause is complete; we will not think of beginning it over again, for that would be an insult to the Savior. "It is finished,"[4] says our Lord Jesus, as He bowed His dear triumphant head and gave up the ghost, and if it is finished, we will not dream of adding to it. It is finished; we have no work to do with the view of self-salvation. But you say to me, "Are we not to work out our own salvation?" Certainly we are. We are to work out our own salvation because God works it in us. It is our own salvation, and we show it forth in our lives: we work it out from within; we develop it from day to day and let men see what the Lord has done for us.

It must first be worked for us and then in us, or we can never work it out. They were assuredly to

---

4. John 19:30.

cease from all sinful work. How can the pardoned man continue in sin? We are done with toiling for the devil now. We will no more waste our lives in his service. Many men are worn to rottenness in the service of their lusts, but the servant of God has been set free from that yoke of bondage. We are slaves no longer: we can quit the hard bondage of Egypt and rest in the Lord.

We are also done with selfish work; we now seek first the kingdom of heaven, and look that all other things shall be added to us by the goodness of our heavenly Father. Henceforth we find rest by bearing the easy yoke of Christ. We have joy to spend and be spent in His beloved service.

He has made us free, and therefore we are under bonds to His love forever. O Lord, I am Thy servant, I am Thy servant; Thou hast loosed my bonds, henceforth I am bound to Thee. God, grant that this may be a high day to Thee because Thou dost gladly realize the grand truths that are shadowed forth in these delightful types. Amen.

23

Christic, Our Life[1]

Christ, who is our life.
—Colossians 3:4

Paul's marvelously rich expression indicates that Christ is the source of our life. "You hath he quickened, who were dead in trespasses and sins."[2] That same voice which brought Lazarus out of the tomb raised us to newness of life. He is now the substance of our spiritual life. It is by His life that we live; He is in us, the hope of glory, the spring of our actions, the central thought which moves every other thought. Christ is the sustenance of our life. What can the Christian feed upon but Jesus's flesh and blood? "This is the bread which cometh down from heaven, that a man may eat thereof, and not die."[3] O wayworn[4] pilgrims in this wilderness of sin, you never get a morsel to satisfy the hunger of your spirits, except when you find it in Him! Christ is the solace of our life. All our true joys come from Him, and in times of trouble, His presence is our consolation.

---

1. From "August 10," *Morning by Morning*, 207–8.
2. Ephesians 2:1.
3. John 6:50.
4. *Wayworn* is an archaic term that means "to be weary from travel."

There is nothing worth living for but Him, and His loving-kindness is better than life!

Christ is the object of our life. As speeds the ship toward the port, so hastens the believer toward the haven of his Savior's bosom. As flies the arrow to its goal, so flies the Christian toward the perfecting of his fellowship with Christ Jesus. As the soldier fights for his captain and is crowned in his captain's victory, so the believer contends for Christ and gets his triumph out of the triumphs of his Master. For him to live is Christ.[5] Christ is the exemplar of our life. Where there is the same life within, there will, there must be, to a great extent the same developments without, and if we live in near fellowship with the Lord Jesus, we shall grow like Him. We shall set Him before us as our divine copy, and we shall seek to tread in His footsteps, until He shall become the crown of our life in glory. Oh! How safe, how honored, how happy is the Christian, since Christ is our life!

---

5. See Philippians 1:21.

24

All but Christ Is Vanity[1]

Behold, all is vanity.
—Ecclesiastes 1:14

Nothing can satisfy the entire man but the Lord's love and the Lord's own self. Saints have tried to anchor in other roadsteads, but they have been driven out of such fatal refuges. Solomon, the wisest of men, was permitted to make experiments for us all and to do for us what we must not dare to do for ourselves. Here is his testimony in his own words:

> So I was great, and increased more than all that were before me in Jerusalem: also my wisdom remained with me. And whatsoever mine eyes desired I kept not from them, I withheld not my heart from any joy; for my heart rejoiced in all my labour: and this was my portion of all my labour. Then I looked on all the works that my hands had wrought, and on the labour that I had laboured to do: and, behold, all was vanity and vexation of spirit, and there was no profit under the sun.[2]

1. From "December 2," *Evening by Evening*, 310–11.
2. Ecclesiastes 2:9–11.

"Vanity of vanities; all is vanity."[3] What! The whole of it is vanity? O favored monarch, is there nothing in all your wealth? Nothing in that wide dominion reaching from the river even to the sea? Nothing in Palmyra's[4] glorious palaces? Nothing in the house of the forest of Lebanon?[5] In all your music and dancing and wine and luxury, is there nothing? "Nothing," he says, "but weariness of spirit." This was his verdict when he had trodden the whole round of pleasure. To embrace our Lord Jesus, to dwell in His love, and to be fully assured of union with Him—this is all in all.

Dear reader, you need not try other forms of life in order to see whether they are better than the Christian's: if you roam around the world, you will see no sights like a sight of the Savior's face; if you could have all the comforts of life, if you lost your Savior, you would be wretched, but if you win Christ, then should you rot in a dungeon, you would find it a paradise; should you live in obscurity or die with famine, you will yet be satisfied with favor and full of the goodness of the Lord.

---

3. Ecclesiastes 1:2.

4. Palmyra was a Roman imperial city located in present-day Syria. The first-century Jewish historian Flavius Josephus (37–ca. 100) identified Palmyra with the ancient city of Tadmor, referenced in 2 Chronicles 8:4, though modern archaeologists dispute this claim. See Trevor Bryce, *Ancient Syria: A Three Thousand Year History* (New York: Oxford University Press, 2004), 276.

5. Ancient Lebanon was forested and was regarded during the Old Testament era for its cedar trees. For references to the cedars of Lebanon, see Psalms 29:5; 92:12; 104:16; Zechariah 11:1.

25

The High Standing of Christ[1]

I will judge of your piety by this barometer: does Christ stand high or low with you? If you have thought little of Christ, if you have been content to live without His presence, if you have cared little for His honor, if you have been neglectful of His laws, then I know that your soul is sick—God grant that it may not be sick unto death! But if the first thought of your spirit has been, how can I honor Jesus? If the daily desire of your soul has been, O that I knew where I might find Him! I tell you that you may have a thousand infirmities and may even scarcely know whether you are a child of God at all, and yet I am persuaded, beyond a doubt, that you are safe, since Jesus is great in your esteem. I care not for your rags; what do you think of *His* royal apparel? I care not for your wounds, though they bleed in torrents; what do you think of *His* wounds? Are they like glittering rubies in your esteem? I think nothing less of you, though you lie like Lazarus[2] on the dunghill and the

---

1. From "The Rose and the Lily," in C. H. Spurgeon, *Flashes of Thought* (London: Passmore and Alabaster, 1874), 460. A sermon from Song of Solomon 2:1 delivered at the Metropolitan Tabernacle on December 8, 1867.

2. This is an allusion to Lazarus's death and subsequent miraculous resurrection at the hand of Jesus. See John 11:1–46.

dogs do lick you; I judge you not by your poverty; what do you think of the King in His beauty? Has He a glorious high throne in your heart? Would you set Him higher if you could? Would you be willing to die if you could but add another trumpet to the strain that proclaims His praise? Ah! Then, it is well with you. Whatever you may think of yourself, if Christ is great to you, you shall be with Him before long.

Metropolitan Tabernacle

C. H. Spurgeon, *C. H. Spurgeon's Autobiography. Compiled from His Diary, Letters, and Records.* Vol. 2. 4 vols (London: Passmore and Alabaster, 1898), 321.

26

Communion with Christ[1]

We have communion with Christ *in His thoughts, views, and purposes,* for His thoughts are our thoughts according to our capacity and sanctity. Believers take the same view of matters as Jesus does; that which pleases Him pleases them and that which grieves Him grieves them also. Consider, for instance, the greatest theme of our thought, and see whether our thoughts are not like those of Christ. He delights in the Father; He loves to glorify the Father. Do not we? Is not the Father the center of our soul's delight? Do we not rejoice at the very sound of His name? Does not our spirit cry, "Abba, Father"?[2] Thus it is clear we feel as Jesus feels toward the Father, and so we have the truest communion with Him. This is but one instance; your contemplations will bring before you a wide variety of topics wherein we think with Jesus. Now, one's judgment, opinion, and purpose forms the highway of communion; yes, it is communion.

We also have communion with Christ *in our emotions.* Have you never felt a holy horror when you have heard a word of blasphemy in the street? Thus Jesus felt when He saw sin and bore it in His own person:

---

1. From "Communion with Christ and His People," *ST* (February 1883), 54–55.

2. Romans 8:15; Galatians 4:6.

only He felt it infinitely more than you do. Have you never felt as you looked upon sinners that you must weep over them? Those are holy tears and contain the same ingredients as those that Jesus shed when He lamented over Jerusalem. Yes, in our zeal for God, our hatred of sin, our detestation of falsehood, our pity for men, we have true communion with Jesus.

Further, we have had fellowship with Christ *in many of our actions*. Have you ever tried to teach the ignorant? This Jesus did. Have you found it difficult? So Jesus found it. Have you striven to reclaim the backslider? Then you were in communion with the Good Shepherd who hastens into the wilderness to find the one lost sheep, finds it, lays it upon His shoulders, and brings it home, rejoicing. Have you ever watched over a soul night and day with tears? Then you have had communion with Him who has borne all our names upon His broken heart and carries the memorial of them upon His pierced hands. Yes, in acts of self-denial, liberality, benevolence, and piety, we enter into communion with Him who went about doing good. Whenever we try to disentangle the snarls of strife and to make peace between men who are at enmity, then are we doing what the great Peacemaker did, and we have communion with the Lord and Giver of peace. Wherever, indeed, we cooperate with the Lord Jesus in His designs of love to men, we are in true and active communion with Him.

27

———— ««◦»» ————

Feasting on Christ by Faith[1]

See what Christ is to us. He is the Paschal Lamb, not a bone of which was broken. You believe it. Come then and act upon your belief by feeding upon Christ; keep the feast in your own souls this day. That sprinkled blood of His has brought you safety: the destroying angel cannot touch you or your house. The Lamb Himself has become your food; feed on Him; remove your spiritual hunger by receiving Jesus into your heart. This is the food whereof if a man eats, he shall live forever. Be filled with all the fullness of God, as you now receive the Lord Jesus as God and man. "Ye are complete in him."[2] Ye are perfect in Jesus Christ.[3] Can you not say of Him: He "is all my salvation, and all my desire"?[4] "Christ is all, and in all."[5]

Do not merely learn this lesson as a doctrine, but enjoy it as a personal experience. Jesus our Passover is slain; let Him be eaten. Let us feast on Him and then be ready to journey through the wilderness, in

---

1. From "On the Cross After Death," *MTP*, 33:202–4. A sermon on John 19:31–37 delivered at the Metropolitan Tabernacle on April 3, 1887.

2. Colossians 2:10.

3. This is likely an allusion to Hebrews 10:14.

4. 2 Samuel 23:5.

5. Colossians 3:11.

the strength of this divine meat, until we come to the promised rest.

We see here the salvation of sinners. Jesus Christ's side is pierced to give to sinners the double cure of sin: the taking away of its guilt and power, but better than this, sinners are to have their hearts broken by a sight of the Crucified. By this means also they are to obtain faith. "They shall look upon me whom they have pierced, and they shall mourn for him."[6] Beloved, our Lord Jesus came not only to save sinners but to seek them; His death not only saves those who have faith, but it creates faith in those who have it not. The cross produces the faith and repentance which it demands. If you cannot come to Christ with faith and repentance, come to Christ for faith and repentance, for He can give them to you. He is pierced on purpose that you may be pricked to the heart. His blood, which freely flows, is shed for many for the remission of sins.[7] What you have to do is just to look, and as you look, those blessed feelings that are the marks of conversion and regeneration shall be accomplished in you by a sight of Him. Oh, blessed lesson!

Put it into practice this morning. Oh, that in this great house many may now have done with self and look to the crucified Savior and find life eternal in Him! For this is the main end of John's writing this record, and this is the chief design of our preaching upon it: we long that you may believe. Come, you guilty—come and trust the Son of God who died for you.

---

6. Zechariah 12:10.
7. This is an allusion to Matthew 26:28.

Come, you foul and polluted, come and wash in this sacred stream poured out for you. There is life in a look at the Crucified One. There is life at this moment for every one of you who will look to Him. God grant you may look and live, for Jesus Christ's sake! Amen.

28

Thirsting for Christ[1]

In the last day, that great day of the feast, Jesus stood and cried, saying, If any man thirst, let him come unto me, and drink.
—John 7:37

Patience had her perfect work in the Lord Jesus, and until the last day of the feast, He pleaded with the Jews, even as, on this last day of the year, He pleads with us and waits to be gracious to us. Admirable indeed is the long-suffering of the Savior in bearing with some of us year after year, notwithstanding our provocations, rebellions, and resistance of His Holy Spirit. Wonder of wonders that we are still in the land of mercy!

Pity expressed herself most plainly, for Jesus cried, which implies not only the loudness of His voice but the tenderness of His tones. He entreats us to be reconciled. "We pray you," says the apostle, "as though God did beseech you by us."[2] What earnest, pathetic terms are these! How deep must be the love which makes the Lord weep over sinners and like a mother woo His children to His bosom! Surely at the call of such a cry, our willing hearts will come.

---

1. From "December 31," *Morning by Morning*, 338–39.
2. 2 Corinthians 5:20.

Provision is made most plenteously; all is provided that man can need to quench his soul's thirst. To his conscience, the atonement brings peace; to his understanding, the gospel brings the richest instruction; to his heart, the person of Jesus is the noblest object of affection; to the whole man, the truth as it is in Jesus supplies the purest nutriment. Thirst is terrible, but Jesus can remove it. Though the soul were utterly famished, Jesus could restore it.

Proclamation is made most freely that every thirsty one is welcome. No other distinction is made but that of thirst. Whether it be the thirst of avarice, ambition, pleasure, knowledge, or rest, he who suffers from it is invited. The thirst may be bad in itself and be no sign of grace but rather a mark of inordinate sin longing to be gratified with deeper draughts of lust, but it is not goodness in the creature which brings him the invitation; the Lord Jesus sends it freely and without respect of persons.

Personality is declared most fully. The sinner must come to Jesus, not to works, ordinances, or doctrines, but to the personal Redeemer, who His own self bore our sins in His own body on the tree. The bleeding, dying, rising Savior is the only star of hope to a sinner. Oh, for grace to come now and drink, before the sun sets upon the year's last day!

No waiting or preparation is so much as hinted at. Drinking represents a reception for which no fitness is required. A fool, a thief, a harlot can drink, and so sinfulness of character is no bar to the invitation to believe in Jesus. We want no golden cup, no bejeweled chalice,[3] in which to convey the water to the thirsty; the mouth of poverty is welcome to stoop down and quaff[4] the flowing flood. Blistered, leprous, filthy lips may touch the stream of divine love; they cannot pollute it but shall themselves be purified. Jesus is the fount of hope. Dear reader, hear the dear Redeemer's loving voice as He cries to each of us, "If any man thirst, let him come unto me, and drink."[5]

---

3. *Chalice* means "a large cup or goblet, normally for drinking wine."

4. *Quaff* is an archaic word meaning "drink."

5. John 7:37.

29

—⊷ ⊶(o)⊷ ⊶—

A Sacrifice of Thanksgiving[1]

Brethren, this ought to be the result of every Christian's experience of divine grace. "O LORD, truly I am thy servant…and the son of thine handmaid: thou hast loosed my bonds. I will offer to thee the sacrifice of thanksgiving."[2] Being delivered from spiritual bondage and made servants of the living God, we must and will praise the Lord as long as we have any being. Thanksgiving should always run parallel with prayer in connection with the church of God. What is true of the individual is true of individuals collected as a corporate body. There is not a true church of God on earth, but what has abundant cause to say, "I will offer the sacrifice of thanksgiving"; and we make a great mistake if, when we hold our days of prayer and cry to God, we do not at the same time make them days of praise and bless His holy name for what we have received. David seems to me in this verse to stand out in contrast with many, for there are some who will say, "I will continue to pray." "Yes," says David, "but I will offer the sacrifice of thanksgiving." Others will say, "We will meet together and sorrow over the sad estate of Zion; we

---

1. C. H. Spurgeon, *Able to the Uttermost: Twenty Gospel Sermons* (Bellingham, Wash.: Logos Bible Software, 2009), 82–83.

2. Psalm 116:16–17.

will speak with one another about the defections of the faithful, the lack of piety, godliness, the superficiality of piety, the heresy of much of the doctrine that is preached, and the worldliness of much of the living that is lived." "Yes," David would say, "and I will come with you, too, and make confession and humble myself before God, but I will also offer the sacrifice of thanksgiving."

There is a tendency in the church of God to play very much upon the discordant strings of the heart rather than those which still remain in tune. David would not forget how much there is that is out of joint. He would be among the first to humble himself before the Lord, among the first to join with Jeremiah and say, "Oh that my head were waters, and mine eyes a fountain of tears, that I might weep day and night for the slain of the daughter of my people";[3] but still he resolves upon it; he declares it against all comers—"I will offer to thee the sacrifice of thanksgiving."

Now, I want you, dear brethren, if at any time you have been inclined to deal out the word of discouragement, or even the more bitter word of censure, all round, upon this church and that church and the other and upon this people of God and the other people of God—instead of that, come to the resolution of the psalmist which now lies before us and say, "With all the church's faults and with all our own, with all that there is to deplore and all that there is to confess, yet from this we will not put aside: we will offer the sacrifice of thanksgiving."

---

3. Jeremiah 9:1.

I make that my resolve tonight, and I do it for four reasons. First, because I believe it is due to God; second, because I believe it is good for myself; third, because I believe it is encouraging to my fellow workers; and fourth, because I think it is one of the helps toward the accomplishment of the purpose we are aiming at.

30

━━━━ ◦((◦)) ◦ ━━━━

The Glory of the Cross[1]

One of Paul's great reasons for glorying in the cross was its action upon himself. What was its effect upon him? The cross is never without influence. Come where it may, it works for life or for death. Wherever there is Christ's cross, there are also two other crosses. On either side there is one, and Jesus is in the midst. Two thieves were crucified with Christ, and Paul tells us their names in his case: "The world is crucified unto me, and I unto the world."[2] Self and the world are both crucified when Christ's cross appears and is believed in. Beloved, what does Paul mean? Does he not mean just this—that ever since he had seen Christ, he looked upon the world as a crucified, hung up, gibbeted[3] thing, which had no more power over Paul than a criminal hung upon a cross?

What power has a corpse on a gibbet? Such power had the world over Paul. The world despised him, and he could not go after the world if he wanted to and would not go after it if he could. He

1. From "The Cross Our Glory," *MTP*, 31:502–3. A sermon on Galatians 6:14 delivered at the Metropolitan Tabernacle on September 13, 1885.

2. Galatians 6:14.

3. A *gibbet* is a post erected for the purpose of hanging condemned criminals.

was dead to it, and it was dead to him; thus there was a double separation.

How does the cross do this? To be under the dominion of this present evil world is horrible; how does the cross help us to escape? Why, brethren, he that has ever seen the cross looks upon the world's pomp and glory as a vain show. The pride of her-aldry and the glitter of honor fade into meanness[4] before the Crucified One. O you great ones, what are your silks and your furs and your jewelry and your gold and your stars and your garters, to one who has learned to glory in Christ crucified! The old clothes which belong to the hangman are quite as precious. The world's light is darkness when the Sun of Righteousness[5] shines from the tree. What care we for all the kingdoms of the world and the glory thereof when once we see the thorn-crowned Lord? There is more glory about one nail of the cross than about all the scepters of all kings. Let the knights of the Golden Fleece meet in chapter, and all the Knights of the Garter stand in their stalls, and what is all their splendor?[6] Their glories wither before the inevitable hour of doom, while the glory of the cross is eternal. Everything of earth grows dull and dim when seen by light of the cross.

So was it with the world's approval. Paul would not ask the world to be pleased with him, since it knew not his Lord, or only knew Him to crucify

---

4. *Mean* is an archaic term for "poor quality or shabby appearance."

5. This is an allusion to Malachi 4:2.

6. These are chivalric orders of knights formed in Spain (Fleece) and England (Garter), respectively, during the late medieval era.

Him. Can a Christian be ambitious to be written down as one of the world's foremost men when that world cast out his Lord? They crucified our Master; shall His servants court their love? Such approval would be all stained with blood. They crucified my Master, the Lord of glory; do I want them to smile on me and say to me, "Reverend Sir" and "Learned Doctor"? No, the friendship of the world is enmity with God,[7] and therefore to be dreaded. Mouths that spit on Jesus shall give me no kisses. Those who hate the doctrine of the atonement hate my life and soul, and I desire not their esteem.

---

7. This is an allusion to James 4:4.

31

The Cross and the World[1]

Paul also saw that the world's wisdom was absurd.
That age talked of being wise and philosophical! Yes,
and its philosophy brought it to crucify the Lord of
glory. It did not know perfection, nor perceive the
beauty of pure unselfishness. To slay the Messiah
was the outcome of the culture of the Pharisee, to
put to death the greatest teacher of all time was the
ripe fruit of Sadducean thought. The cogitations of
the present age have performed no greater feat than
to deny the doctrine of satisfaction for sin.

They have crucified our Lord afresh by their crit-
icisms and their new theologies, and this is all the
world's wisdom ever does. Its wisdom lies in scatter-
ing doubt, quenching hope, and denying certainty,
and therefore the wisdom of the world to us is sheer
folly. This century's philosophy will one day be
spoken of as an evidence that softening of the brain
was very usual among its scientific men. We count
the thought of the present moment to be methodical
madness, Bedlam[2] out of doors, and those who are

---

1. From "The Cross Our Glory," *MTP*, 31:503–4. A sermon on
Galatians 6:14 delivered at the Metropolitan Tabernacle on September 13, 1885.

2. In context, Bedlam was a nickname for the Bethlehem Royal
Hospital, which was established in London in the thirteenth century

furthest gone in it are credulous beyond imagination. God has poured contempt upon the wise men of this world; their foolish hearts are blinded; they grope at noonday.

So, too, the apostle saw the world's religion to be nothing. It was the world's religion that crucified Christ; the priests were at the bottom of it, the Pharisees urged it on. The church of the nation, the church of many ceremonies, the church which loved the traditions of the elders, the church of phylacteries[3] and broad-bordered garments—it was this church, which, acting by its officers, crucified the Lord. Paul therefore looked with pity upon priests and altars and upon all the attempts of a Christless world to make up by finery of worship for the absence of the Spirit of God. Once one sees Christ on the cross, architecture and fine display become meretricious,[4] tawdry things. The cross calls for worship in spirit and in truth, and the world knows nothing of this.

And so it was with the world's pursuits. Some ran after honor, some toiled after learning, others labored for riches, but to Paul these were all trifles since he had seen Christ on the cross. He that has seen Jesus die will never go into the toy business; he puts away childish things.

---

as the first insane asylum. The word *bedlam* has subsequently come to mean "uproar or confusion."

3. A *phylactery* is a small box containing Hebrew texts worn by Jewish men while praying as a reminder to observe the law. The practice has precedent in the Pentateuch. See Exodus 13:9; Deuteronomy 6:8; 11:18.

4. *Meretricious* means "to be outwardly attractive but devoid of real value or integrity."

A child, a pipe, a little soap, and many pretty bubbles: such is the world.

The cross alone can wean us from such play. And so it was with the world's pleasures and with the world's power. The world and everything that belonged to the world had become as a corpse to Paul, and he was as a corpse to it. See where the corpse swings in chains on the gibbet. What a foul, rotten thing! We cannot endure it! Do not let it hang longer above ground to fill the air with pestilence. Let the dead be buried out of sight. The Christ that died upon the cross now lives in our hearts. The Christ who took human guilt has taken possession of our souls, and henceforth we live only in Him, for Him, by Him. He has engrossed our affections. All our ardors burn for Him. God make it to be so with us, that we may glorify God and bless our age.

Negretti and Zambra, "Seated Portrait of Charles and Susanna Spurgeon with Hats." n.d., photograph card, 4.125 x 2 in. Published by Passmore and Alabaster, London. Held at The Spurgeon Library, Midwestern Baptist Theological Seminary, Kansas City, Missouri.

32

Forgetting Christ[1]

It appears almost impossible that those who have
been redeemed by the blood of the dying Lamb
should ever forget their Ransomer, that those who
have been loved with an everlasting love by the eternal Son of God should ever forget that Son, but if
startling to the ear, it is alas, too apparent to the eye
to allow us to deny the fact. Forget Him who never
forgot us! Forget Him who poured His blood forth for
our sins! Forget Him who loved us even to the death!
Can it be possible? Yes, it is not only possible, but
conscience confesses that it is too sadly a fault of all
of us that we can remember anything except Christ.
The object which we should make the monarch of
our hearts is the very thing we are most inclined to
forget. Where one would think that memory would
linger and unmindfulness would be an unknown
intruder, that is the spot which is desecrated by the
feet of forgetfulness and that the place where memory too seldom looks. I appeal to the conscience of
every Christian here: Can you deny the truth of what
I utter? Do you not find yourselves forgetful of Jesus?
Some creature steals away your heart, and you are

---

1. "The Remembrance of Christ," *NPSP*, 1:9–10. A sermon from
1 Corinthians 11:24 delivered at New Park Street Chapel on January
7, 1855.

unmindful of Him upon whom your affection ought to be set. Some earthly business engrosses your attention when you should have your eye steadily fixed upon the cross. It is the incessant round of world, world, world; the constant din of earth, earth, earth, that takes away the soul from Christ.

The cause of this is very apparent: it lies in one or two facts. We forget Christ, because regenerate persons as we really are, still, corruption and death remain even in the regenerate. We forget Him because we carry about with us the old Adam of sin and death. If we were purely newborn creatures, we should never forget the name of Him whom we love. If we were entirely regenerated beings, we should sit down and meditate on all our Savior did and suffered, on all He is, on all He has gloriously promised to perform, and never would our roving affections stray, but centered, nailed, fixed eternally to one object, we should continually contemplate the death and sufferings of our Lord. But alas! We have a worm in the heart, a pesthouse,[2] a charnel house within, lusts, vile imaginations, and strong evil passions, which, like wells of poisonous water, send out continually streams of impurity. I have a heart, which God knows I wish I could wring from my body and hurl to an infinite distance; a soul which is a cave of unclean birds, a den of loathsome creatures, where dragons haunt and owls do congregate, where every evil beast of ill-omen dwells; a heart too vile to have a parallel—"deceitful above all things,

---

2. A *pesthouse* was a house used for recovery from serious illness, especially the plague.

and desperately wicked."[3] This is the reason why I am forgetful of Christ.

Nor is this the sole cause. I suspect it lies somewhere else too. We forget Christ because there are so many other things around us to attract our attention. "But," you say, "they ought not to do so, because though they are around us, they are nothing in comparison with Jesus Christ; though they are in dread proximity to our hearts, what are they compared with Christ?" But do you know, dear friends, that the nearness of an object has a very great effect upon its power? The sun is many, many times larger than the moon, but the moon has a greater influence upon the tides of the ocean than the sun, simply because it is nearer and has a greater power of attraction. So I find that a little crawling worm of the earth has more effect upon my soul than the glorious Christ in heaven; a handful of golden earth, a puff of fame, a shout of applause, a thriving business, my house, my home, will affect me more than all the glories of the upper world, yes, than the beatific vision itself, simply because earth is near and heaven is far away. Happy day, when I shall be borne aloft on angels' wings to dwell forever near my Lord, to bask in the sunshine of His smile, and to be lost in the ineffable radiance of His lovely countenance. We see then the cause of forgetfulness; let us blush over it; let us be sad that we neglect our Lord so much, and now let us attend to His word, "This do in remembrance of me,"[4] hoping that its solemn sounds may charm away the demon of base ingratitude.

---

3. Jeremiah 17:9
4. 1 Corinthians 11:24

33

Sensitivity to Sin[1]

I believe that in many Christians, the sense of sin is much stronger ten years after they have been saved than it is at the time of their conversion. There is not any despair mixed with it, and the fear of punishment has gone, but a sense of horror at the terrible guilt of sin will sometimes come over a Christian who is far advanced in the divine life; nay, the further he is advanced in the divine life, the more will horror take hold of him whenever he sees sin, even in others, and still more in himself. Some glib professors[2] talk of having got out of Romans 7; I hope they will grow in grace until they get into Romans 7! It seems to me as if they were in Romans 1, so they have a long way to travel before they will get into Romans 7. The nearer you get to perfection, the more horrified you feel because of the sin that still remains in you; and the more horror you feel at your sin, the more intense will be your gratitude to the bleeding Savior who has put that sin away, and, in consequence, the more intense will be your love to Him.

---

1. From "Who Loves Christ Most?," *MTP*, 50:114–15. A sermon on Luke 7:41–43 delivered at the Metropolitan Tabernacle on February 3, 1876.

2. In context, this term refers to those who profess faith in Christ but are at least potentially nominal or false believers.

I charge you, Christian people, if you want your piety to be increased, never to blunt your sensibility of sin. Do not begin to look at sin in any light which takes away any of its blackness. The devil himself is not so bad as sin is, for it is sin that made the devil. Satan was a holy angel until sin came into him, but sin itself was never anything else but sin, a horrible thing, and it never will be anything else but sin; look at it in whatever way you may. Some have spoken of sin as being merely a failure or a slight slip. God keep you, beloved, from ever using such language as that! Sin, in a child of God, is a damnable thing—as damnable as it is most atrociously wicked—and if it were not for the grace of God, which takes it away, the brightest saint would soon be banished from God's presence. Sin is always an evil thing, but in a child of God it is a worse thing than in world-lings, for he sins against greater light and knowledge than they possess.

Brethren and sisters in Christ, if you desire to cultivate, as I trust you do, the feeling that you did owe your Lord five hundred pence, which He has freely forgiven you, *you must often think of the spirituality of the law of God.*

34

---- ⇒►•◄(•)►•◄⇐ ----

Hypocrisy[1]

Hypocrisy is *useless* altogether, for God sees through it. You may by great cleverness delude your fellow men for a while, though you will find it a poor and difficult business, but you can never deceive God. It is not that you may deceive the Lord for a little time and then afterward be discovered. No, you cannot mislead Him, even for an instant. He reads us as we read a book. He sees through us as we see through a sheet of clear glass. The instantaneous imagination which flits across the mind like a stray bird, leaving no track or trace, God observes it and knows it altogether. To pretend to be other than we are before God is hideous madness. Surely, Satan himself must laugh in his sleeve at those who come before God with words of piety on their lips when there is no devotion in their hearts: it is the comedy of a tragic blasphemy. It is utterly useless. It is a waste of time and energy. It would be infinitely better if you were to do something else than dress and paint and put on ornaments to go before God, who sees you in your spiritual death to be nothing but naked corruption. May God grant that we may never play the fool in

---

1. From "Truthfulness," *MTP*, 27:112–13. A sermon from Jeremiah 5:3 delivered at the Metropolitan Tabernacle.

this way, for playing the fool is to hope to appear otherwise before Him than what we really are deep down in our hearts.

Nor is it only useless; it is *injurious*. For any man to hope that he can stand better with God by speaking more softly than his heart would suggest or by using words that his soul does not really enter into is to be doing the reverse of what he thinks to do. You spoil your sacrifice if there is any tincture[2] of the odious gall of hypocrisy about it. Oh, if the Pharisee did but know that when he made broad the borders of his garments and put on his phylactery and sounded a trumpet before him in the streets, he was not pleasing God but was actually provoking Him; surely he would have sense enough to mend his ways. Everything about you and me that is unreal, God hates, and hates it more in His own people than anywhere else. If in prayer we use expressions that really do not come from our hearts, or if in talking to our fellow men we stick feathers in our caps to be a little taller and finer than we really are, it is abhorrent in the sight of God. He would sooner have us come before Him in all the nakedness and shame of our first parents and stand there and confess our crime, than dress ourselves in the fig leaves of formality and hypocrisy. Pretense is injurious to men as well as useless: it is not only an empty wind, but it is as the breath of pestilence.

Moreover, pretense is *deadening*, for he that begins with tampering with truth will, as I have already shown you, go on from bad to worse. He may say at

---

2. A *tincture* is a medicine made by dissolving a drug in alcohol.

first, "Is your servant a dog, that he should do this thing?" and yet, like a dog, he will go into all manner of filthiness before he is done. Let a man once begin to tamper with his conscience, to play tricks with words, and especially to trifle with the solemnities of religion, and there is no knowing what he will be. Oh, I charge my tongue, as I charge yours, never to use a word which is not true when speaking with God or for God, for falsehood before the Judge of all the earth is blasphemy. When we think of Him in our secret souls, we must be careful not to allow a false idea, for it is dreadful even to think untruth before God. Falsehood in common life must not be tolerated for a moment. Once you begin to sail by the wind of policy and trickery, you must tack[3] and then tack again and again; and as surely as you are alive, you will yet have to tack again; but if you have the motive force of truth within you, as a steamboat has its own engine, then you can go straight in the teeth of wind and tempest. The man of truth is the true man. That is the man to honor God in life and death. That is the man to fear nothing and win everything. He is the man whom the Lord accepts, who feels that if the heavens fall it is not for him to prop them up with a lie if that could make them stand. He is the man who is resolved to be before God and before man just what he is, wearing his heart upon his sleeve and throwing back every shutter of his soul that the divine eye may inspect all! Blessed is the

---

3. *Tack* is a sailing term that means "to change the direction of the vessel so that the wind is shifted from one side to the other in an effort to stay on course."

man whose transgression is forgiven, whose sin is covered, "in whose spirit there is no guile."[4] This freedom from guile is a main ingredient of the blessedness. The conscience must be clear and honest, or it will gather dust and defilement every day, and the man will wax worse and worse.

---

4. Psalm 32:2.

35

Hindering Revival[1]

With these words of caution, I shall now gather up my strength and with all my might labor to stir you up to seek of God a great revival of religion throughout the length and breadth of this land.

Men, brethren and fathers, the Lord God has sent us a blessing. One blessing is the earnest of many. Drops precede the April showers. The mercies which He has already bestowed upon us are but the forerunners and the preludes of something greater and better yet to come. He has given us the former, let us seek of Him the latter rain that His grace may be multiplied among us and His glory may be increased. There are some of you to whom I address myself this morning who stand in the way of any revival of religion. I would affectionately admonish you and beseech you not to impede the Lord's own work. There are some of you, perhaps, here present today who are not consistent in your living. And yet you are professors of religion; you take the sacramental cup into your hand and drink its sacred wine, but still you live as worldlings live and are as carnal and as covetous as they. Oh, my

---

1. From "The Great Revival," *NPSP*, 4:167–68. A sermon on Isaiah 52:10 delivered March 28, 1858, at the Music Hall.

brother, you are a serious drawback to the church's increase. God will never bless an unholy people, and in proportion to our unholiness, He will withhold the blessing from us. Tell me of a church that is inconsistent, and you shall tell me of a church that is unblessed. God will first sweep the house before He will come to dwell in it. He will have His church pure before He will bless it with all the blessings of His grace. Remember that, you inconsistent ones, and turn to God and ask to be rendered holy.

There are others of you who are so coldhearted that you stand in the way of all progress. You are a skid upon the wheels of the church. It cannot move for you. If we would be earnest, you put your cold hand on everything that is bold and daring. You are not prudent and zealous; if you were so, we would bless God for giving you that prudence, which is a jewel for which we ought ever to thank God, if we have a prudent man among us. But there are some of you to whom I allude, who are prudent, but you are cold. You have no earnestness; you do not labor for Christ; you do not serve Him with all your strength. And there are others of you who are imprudent enough to push others on but never go forward yourselves.

O you Laodiceans, you that are neither hot nor cold, remember what the Lord has said of you—"So then, because thou art lukewarm, and neither cold nor hot, I will spue[2] thee out of my mouth."[3] And

---

2. *Spue* is an archaic spelling of the word *spew*.

3. The reference to Laodiceans comes from the letter to the church in Laodicea in Revelation 3:14–22. The Scripture quotation comes from Revelation 3:16.

so He will do with you. Take heed, take heed, you are not only hurting yourselves, but you are injuring the church.

And then there are others of you who are such sticklers for order, so given to everything that has been, that you do not care for any revival, for fear we should hurt you. You would not have the church repaired, lest we should touch one piece of the venerable moss that coats it. You would not cleanse your own garment because there is ancient dirt upon it. You think that because a thing is ancient, therefore it must be venerable. You are lovers of the antique. You would not have a road mended because your grandfather drove his wagon along the rut that is there. "Let it always be there," you say. "Let it always be knee-deep." Did not your grandfather go through it when it was knee-deep with mud, and why should not you do the same? It was good enough for him, and it is good enough for you. You always have taken an easy seat in the chapel. You never saw a revival; you do not want to see it. You believe it is all nonsense and that it is not to be desired. You look back; you find no precedent for it. Doctor So-and-So did not talk about it. Your venerable minister who is dead did not talk, so you say therefore it is not needed. We need not tell you it is scriptural, that you do not care for. It is not orderly, you say. We need not tell you the thing is right; you care more about the thing being ancient than being good. Ah, you will have to get out of the way now; it isn't any good; you may try to stop us, but we will run over you if you do not get out of the way. With a little warning we shall have to run over your prejudices and incur your anger. But your prejudices must not, cannot, restrain us. The prisoner is always happy to break free from his chains, and no matter how your fetters may shackle us, we will dash them in pieces if they stand in the way of the progress of the kingdom of Christ.

36

Confession of Sin[1]

I prefer, however, dear friends, to spend the few minutes remaining to me in recalling to our minds our own *personal sins*. These are sins for which our penitence is most required and for which it is most effectual. We cannot vanquish widespread social sins, but by God's grace we can overcome our own. It may be idle for an obscure individual to lift the lash against a nation, but the least of us may scourge his own homeborn sin and hope for a good result from the chastisement.

Let us personally prostrate ourselves at the feet of our Lord Jesus. Let us recollect that many of us may be much more guilty than may appear from our outward lives. Our secret sins, our heart sins, our sins of omission, must be taken into account. It may have been impossible for some of us to have sinned as others have done; let us now take credit to ourselves on that account. The dog is not to be praised for not straying if it has been chained up. If we have done evil as we could, we need not glory that we have not done that which was impossible for us. Sins of thought, of desire, and of word are also to be put down in our statement, together with all our

1. From "Confession of Sin," *ST* (February 1886): 80–81.

ingratitude to God and want of love for our neighbor and our pride and self-seeking and discontentment.

Let no one of us ever think of compounding[2] for sins which he has committed by the reflection that he has not fallen so grievously as others. We may be very respectable people, and yet we may, in some respects, exceed in sin those who appear to be greater sinners. What if I am not unchaste, yet Pharisaic pride may make me quite as obnoxious to Almighty God. What if I am not a gambler, yet a malicious mind will as surely shut me out of heaven. What if I am not a blasphemer, yet the carnal mind is enmity against God, and if my nature is not changed, I am not reconciled to God. Therefore, it becomes each one to look narrowly within, by hearty self-examination, and after doing so, it will be the wisdom of each one to cry, with penitent David, "Have mercy upon me, O God, according to thy lovingkindness: according unto the multitude of thy tender mercies blot out my transgressions."[3]

Since I am a believer in the Lord Jesus Christ, I know assuredly, at this moment, that all my sins are forgiven me. As to the pardon of every true believer there can be no doubt, if we believe the testimony of Holy Scripture. But we must never dare to quit the place of the publican, who cried, "God be merciful to me a sinner!"[4]

---

2. *Compounding* is an archaic term that meant "escaping prosecution due to a financial payment or similar arrangement."

3. Psalm 51:1.

4. Luke 18:13.

37

—⊷ «•»⊷—

Deliverance to Captives[1]

To preach deliverance to the captives.
—Luke 4:18

None but Jesus can give deliverance to captives. Real liberty comes from Him only. It is a liberty righteously bestowed, for the Son, who is heir of all things, has a right to make men free. The saints honor the justice of God, which now secures their salvation. It is a liberty that has been dearly purchased. Christ speaks it by His power, but He bought it by His blood. He makes you free, but it is by His own bonds. You go clear because He bore your burden for you: you are set at liberty because He has suffered in your stead. But, though dearly purchased, He freely gives it. Jesus asks nothing of us as a preparation for this liberty. He finds us sitting in sackcloth and ashes and bids us put on the beautiful array of freedom; He saves us just as we are, and all without our help or merit.

When Jesus sets free, the liberty is perpetually entailed; no chains can bind again. Let the Master say to me, "Captive, I have delivered you," and it is done forever. Satan may plot to enslave us, but if the

---

1. From "November 25," *Morning by Morning*, 304–5.

Lord be on our side, whom shall we fear? The world, with its temptations, may seek to ensnare us, but mightier is He who is for us than all they who are against us.[2] The machinations of our own deceitful hearts may harass and annoy us, but He who has begun the good work in us will carry it on and perfect it to the end.[3] The foes of God and the enemies of man may gather their hosts together and come with concentrated fury against us, but if God acquits, who is he that condemns? No more free is the eagle that mounts to his rocky aerie and afterward outsoars the clouds than the soul that Christ has delivered. If we are no more under the law but free from its curse, let our liberty be practically exhibited in our serving God with gratitude and delight. "I am thy servant, and the son of thine handmaid: thou hast loosed my bonds."[4] "Lord, what wilt thou have me to do?"[5]

---

2. This is an allusion to Romans 8:31.
3. This is an allusion to Philippians 1:6.
4. Psalm 116:16.
5. Acts 9:6.

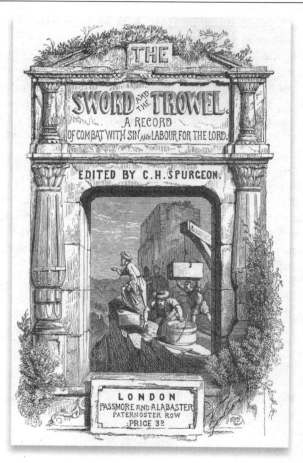

Sword and Trowel Facsimile

C. H. Spurgeon, *C. H. Spurgeon's Autobiography. Compiled from His Diary, Letters, and Records*. Vol. 3. 4 vols (London: Passmore and Alabaster, 1899), 309.

38

—•‹(•)›•—

Godly and Ungodly Anger[1]

God said to Jonah, Doest thou well to be angry?
—Jonah 4:9

Anger is not always or necessarily sinful, but it has such a tendency to run wild that whenever it displays itself, we should be quick to question its character with this inquiry, "Doest thou well to be angry?"[2] It may be that we can answer, "Yes." Very frequently, anger is the madman's firebrand, but sometimes it is Elijah's fire from heaven. We do well when we are angry with sin because of the wrong which it commits against our good and gracious God, or with ourselves because we remain so foolish after so much divine instruction, or with others when the sole cause of anger is the evil which they do. He who is not angry at transgression becomes a partaker in it. Sin is a loathsome and hateful thing, and no renewed heart can patiently endure it. God Himself is angry with the wicked every day, and it is written in His Word, "Ye that love the LORD, hate evil."[3] Far more frequently it is to be feared that our anger is not commendable or even justifiable, and then we

---

1. From "July 13," *Morning by Morning*, 182–83.
2. Jonah 4:4, 9.
3. Psalm 97:10.

must answer, "No." Why should we be fretful with children, passionate with servants, and wrathful with companions? Is such anger honorable to our Christian profession or glorifying to God? Is it not the old evil heart seeking to gain dominion, and should we not resist it with all the might of our newborn nature? Many professors give way to their tempers as though it were useless to attempt resistance, but let the believer remember that he must be a conqueror in every point, or else he cannot be crowned. If we cannot control our tempers, what has grace done for us?... We must not make natural infirmity an excuse for sin, but we must fly to the cross and pray the Lord will crucify our tempers and renew us in gentleness and meekness after His own image.

39

Good Works[1]

Good works are of use to a Christian as an adornment.
You will all remember that passage in the Scriptures
that tells us how a woman should adorn herself:
"Whose adorning let it not be that outward adorning of plaiting the hair, and of wearing of gold, or of
putting on of apparel; but let it be the hidden man of
the heart, in that which is not corruptible, even the
ornament of a meek and quiet spirit."[2] The adornment of good works, the adornment in which we
hope to enter heaven, is the blood and righteousness
of Jesus Christ; but the adornment of a Christian
here below is his holiness, his piety, his consistency.
If some people had a little more piety, they would
not require such a showy dress; if they had a little
more godliness, to set them off, they would have no
need whatever to be always decorating themselves.
The best earrings that a woman can wear are the
earrings of hearing the Word with attention. The
very best ring that we can have upon our finger is
the ring which the father puts upon the finger of the
prodigal son when he is brought back, and the very
best dress we can ever wear is a garment made by the

---

1. From "Good Works," *NPSP*, 2:133–34. A sermon on Titus 2:14
delivered at New Park Street Chapel on March 16, 1856.
2. 1 Peter 3:3–4.

Holy Spirit, the garment of a consistent conduct. But it is marvelous, while many are taking all the trouble they can to array this poor body, they have very few ornaments for their soul; they forgot to dress the soul. Oh no! They are too late at chapel, all because of that other pin, which they might have left out. They come here just when the service is beginning because, indeed, they have so much to put on, they could not be expected to be here in time. And there are Christian men and Christian women who forget what God has written in His Word, which is as true now as ever it was, that Christian women should array themselves with modesty. It would be a good thing, perhaps, if we went back to Wesley's rule, to come out from the world in our apparel and to dress as plainly and neatly as the Quakers, though alas, they have sadly gone from their primitive simplicity. I am obliged to depart a little sometimes from what we call the high things of the gospel, for really the children of God cannot now be told by outward appearance from the children of the devil, and they really ought to be. There should be some distinction between the one and the other, and although religion allows distinction of rank and dress, yet everything in the Bible cries out against our arraying ourselves and making ourselves proud by reason of the goodliness of our apparel.

Some will say, "I wish you would leave that alone!" Of course you do, because it applies to yourself. But we let nothing alone that we believe to be in the Scriptures, and while I would not spare any man's soul, honesty to every man's conscience and honesty to myself demands that I should always speak of that which I see to be an evil breaking out in the church. We should always take care that in everything we keep as near as possible to the written Word. If you want ornaments, here they are. Here are jewels, rings, dresses, and all kinds of ornaments; men and women, you may dress yourselves up till you shine like angels. How can you do it? By dressing yourselves in benevolence, in love to the saints, in honesty and integrity, in uprightness, in godliness, in brotherly kindness, in charity. These are the ornaments that angels themselves admire and that even the world will admire, for men must give admiration to the man or the woman who is arrayed in the jewels of a holy life and godly conversation. I beseech you, brethren, "adorn the doctrine of God our Saviour in all things."[3]

---

3. Titus 2:10.

40

You Shall Be My Witnesses[1]

And ye shall be witnesses unto me.
—Acts 1:8

In order to learn how to discharge your duty as a witness for Christ, look at His example. He is always witnessing: by the well of Samaria or in the temple of Jerusalem, by the lake of Gennesaret or on the mountain's brow.[2] He is witnessing night and day; His mighty prayers are as vocal to God as His daily services. He witnesses under all circumstances; scribes and Pharisees cannot shut His mouth; even before Pilate, He witnesses a good confession.[3] He witnesses so clearly and distinctly that there is no mistake in Him. Christian, make your life a clear testimony. Be you as the brook wherein you may see every stone at the bottom—not as the muddy creek, of which you only see the surface—but clear and

---

1. From "November 7," *Evening by Evening*, 286–87.

2. These are locations from Jesus's earthly ministry. See John 4:1–42 (well of Samaria); Matthew 21:12–17; John 2:13–22 (cleansing the temple); Matthew 14:34–36; Mark 6:53–56 (Gennesaret); Matthew 5–7 (Sermon on the Mount).

3. The scribes and Pharisees were constant adversaries of Jesus in the Gospels. For Jesus's confession before Pilate, see Matthew 27:11–26; Mark 15:1–15; Luke 23:1–7; 13–25; John 18:28–40.

transparent, so that your heart's love to God and man may be visible to all. You need not say, "I am true"; be true. Boast not of integrity, but be upright. So shall your testimony be such that men cannot help seeing it. Never, for fear of feeble man, restrain your witness. Your lips have been warmed with a coal from the altar;[4] let them speak as like heaven-touched lips should do. "In the morning sow thy seed, and in the evening withhold not thine hand."[5] Watch not the clouds, consult not the wind—in season and out of season,[6] witness for the Savior, and if it shall come to pass that for Christ's sake and the gospel's you shall endure suffering in any shape, shrink not but rejoice in the honor thus conferred upon you, that you are counted worthy to suffer with your Lord;[7] and have joy also in this—that your sufferings, losses, and persecutions shall make you a platform, from which more vigorously and with greater power you shall witness for Christ Jesus.

Study your great Exemplar, and be filled with His Spirit. Remember that you need much teaching, much upholding, much grace, and much humility, if your witnessing is to be to your Master's glory.

---

4. This is an allusion to Isaiah 6:6–7.
5. Ecclesiastes 11:6.
6. This is an allusion to 2 Timothy 4:2.
7. This is an allusion to Acts 5:41.

41

Praying for Our Children[1]

I have heard of a father, who used to pray much for the conversion of his sons and daughters, yet he did not see one of them saved. When he came to die, his family had all grown up, and they had themselves become the heads of other households. He sent for them to come to his bedside, and he prayed very earnestly that he might die so joyful and triumphant a death that they might be convinced of the beauty and power of vital godliness and seek the Savior for themselves. That was his plan of bringing his family to Jesus, but it pleased the Lord to allow him to be in great pain of body and much distress of mind; indeed, he was in such anguish of heart that his testimony to the power of grace was of a very negative character. He had no songs of triumph, but he had many moans of pain and many questions about his spiritual state. God puts many of His children to bed in the dark, but they are His children all the same. It is of the wicked that it is written, "There are no bands in their death: but their strength is firm. They

1. From "The Free-Agency of Christ," *MTP*, 50:343–44. A sermon from Mark 8:22–26 delivered on July 18, 1876, at the Metropolitan Tabernacle.

are not in trouble as other men; neither are they plagued like other men."[2]

God's best servants often pass away under a cloud, and it was so with the friend of whom I am speaking. One of his last utterances was the expression of his intense regret that his sons would be confirmed in their unbelief by his experience in his dying hour, yet mark what really happened. They all knew of his genuine piety. They had not a doubt about that matter, for they reckoned him to be one of the best of men, and as they gathered in the house after the funeral, the eldest son said to them, "Brothers and sisters, our father died a very sad death, yet we know that his soul was saved. We all know that he trusted Christ as his Savior and that he lived a most godly life. Now," said he, "if such a man as our father found it hard to die, think how much harder it will be for us if we have to die without a Savior." The same thought had occurred to the rest of the family, and it was not long before they all sought and found their father's God and Savior. You see, the Lord really heard his prayer and granted him the desire of his heart, though not in the way he expected, and He will hear you, my brother, and He will hear you, my sister, but the answer may not come in your way. The Lord has His own way of doing His own work, and sometimes He adopts very singular methods to teach us that there is no power in the method He uses but that all the power lies in Himself.

---

2. Psalm 73:4–5.

42

Personal Evangelism[1]

Piety must begin at home as well as charity. Conversion should begin with those who are nearest to us in ties of relationship. I stir you up, not to be attempting missionary labors for India, not to be casting eyes of pity across to Africa, not to be occupied so much with tears for popish and heathen lands, as for your own children, your own flesh and blood, your own neighbors, your own acquaintances. Lift up your cry to heaven *for them*, and then afterward you shall preach among the nations. Andrew goes to Cappadocia in his afterlife,[2] but he began with his brother, and you shall labor where you please in years to come, but first of all your own household, first of all those who are under your own shadow must receive your guardian care. Be wise in this thing: use the ability you have and use it among those who are near at hand.

Perhaps somebody will be saying, "How did Andrew persuade Simon Peter to come to Christ?" He did so, first, by narrating his own personal

---

1. C. H. Spurgeon, *Words of Counsel for Christian Workers* (Bellingham, Wash.: Logos Bible Software, 2009), 10–12.

2. Spurgeon is referring to the tradition that Andrew was an apostle to Cappadocia, which roughly coincides with present-day Turkey. Some Christian groups consider Andrew to be the first bishop or patriarch of Constantinople.

experience: he said, "We have found the Messia[h]."[3]
What you have experienced of Christ tell to others.
He did so next by intelligently explaining to him
what it was he had found. He did not say he had
found someone who had impressed him but he knew
not who he was; he told him he had found the Messiah, that is, Christ. Be clear in your knowledge of
the gospel and your experience of it, and then tell the
good news to those whose souls you seek. Andrew
had power over Peter because of his own decided
conviction. He did not say, "I hope I have found
Christ," but, "I have found Him." He was sure of
that. Get full assurance of your own salvation. There
is no weapon like it. He that speaks doubtingly of
what he would convince another asks that other to
doubt his testimony. Be positive in your experience
and your assurance, for this will help you.

Andrew had power over Peter because he put the
good news before him in an earnest fashion. He did
not say to him as though it were a commonplace fact,
"The Messiah has come," but no, he communicated
it to him as the most weighty of all messages with
becoming tones and gestures, I doubt not: "We have
found the Messiah, which is called Christ." To your
own kinsfolk, tell your belief, your enjoyments, and
your assurance, tell all judiciously with assurance of
the truth of it, and who can tell whether God may not
bless your work?

Andrew won a soul, won his brother's soul, won
such a treasure! He won no other than that Simon
Peter, who at the first cast of the gospel net, when

3. John 1:41.

Christ had made him a soul-fisherman, caught three thousand souls at a single haul! Peter, a very prince in the Christian church, one of the mightiest of the servants of the Lord in all his usefulness, would be a comfort to Andrew. I should not wonder but what Andrew would say in days of doubt and fear: "Blessed be God that He has made Peter so useful! Blessed be God that ever I spoke to Peter! What I cannot do, Peter will help to do, and while I sit down in my helplessness, I can feel thankful that my dear brother Peter is honored in bringing souls to Christ." Your fingers are yet to wake to ecstasy the living lyre of a heart that up till now has not been tuned to the praise of Christ; you are to kindle the fire that shall light up a sacred sacrifice of a consecrated life to Christ. Only be up and doing for the Lord Jesus, be importunate and prayerful, be zealous and self-sacrificing. I make no doubt of it that when we have proved our God by prayer, He will pour down such a blessing that we shall not have room to receive it.

43

A Christless Sermon[1]

So we can say of Jesus Christ, that we had rather hear the repetitions of Jesus than any novelty from any preacher whatsoever. O how our souls are dissatisfied when we listen to a sermon destitute of Christ. There are some preachers who can manage to deliver a sermon and leave out Christ's name altogether. Surely the true believer will stand like Mary Magdalene over the sermon and say: "They have taken away my LORD, and I know not where they have laid him."[2] Take away Christ from the sermon, and you have taken away its essence. The marrow of theology is Christ, the very bone and sinew of the gospel is preaching Christ. A Christless sermon is the merriment of hell. A Christless sermon is a fearful waste of time; it incurs the blood of souls and dyes that man's skirts with gore who dares to preach it. But too much of Christ we cannot have. Give us Christ always, Christ ever. The monotony of Christ is sweet variety, and even the unity of Christ has in it all the elements of harmony. Christ, on His cross and on His throne, in the manger and in the tomb—

---

1. From Spurgeon, "A Visit to Calvary," *Spurgeon's Sermons*, 2:329–30.
2. John 20:13.

Christ everywhere is sweet to us. We love His name; we adore His person; we delight to hear of His works. Come, then, to Calvary awhile with me, that there I may say to you as Pilate did in his palace: "Behold the man!"[3]

---

3. John 19:5.

Silver Wedding

C. H. Spurgeon, *C. H. Spurgeon's Autobiography. Compiled from His Diary, Letters, and Records.* Vol. 4. 4 vols (London: Passmore and Alabaster, 1900), 23.

44

Preaching for Conversion[1]

Preach very solemnly, for it is a weighty business, but let your matter be lively and pleasing, for this will prevent solemnity from souring into dreariness. Be so thoroughly solemn that all your faculties are aroused and consecrated, and then a dash of humor will only add more intense gravity to the discourse, even as a flash of lightning makes midnight darkness all the more impressive. Preach to one point, concentrating all your energies upon the object aimed at. There must be no riding of hobbies, no introduction of elegancies of speech, no suspicion of personal display, or you will fail. Sinners are quick-witted people and soon detect even the smallest effort to glorify self. Forego everything for the sake of those you long to save. Be a fool for Christ's sake if this will win them, or be a scholar if that will be more likely to impress them. Spare neither labor in the study, prayer in the closet, nor zeal in the pulpit. If men do not judge their souls to be worth a thought, compel them to see that their minister is of a very different opinion.

Desire to see conversions, expect them, and prepare for them. Resolve that your hearers shall either

1. From C. H. Spurgeon, *Lectures to My Students: Addresses Delivered to the Students of the Pastors' College*, Metropolitan Tabernacle, second series (New York: Robert Carter and Brothers, 1889), 2:278–79.

yield to your Lord or be without excuse and that this shall be the immediate result of the sermon now in hand. Do not let the Christians around you wonder when souls are saved, but urge them to believe in the undiminished power of the glad tidings, and teach them to marvel if no saving result follows the delivery of the testimony of Jesus. Do not permit sinners to hear sermons as a matter of course or allow them to play with the edged tools of Scripture as if they were mere toys, but again and again remind them that every true gospel sermon leaves them worse if it does not make them better. Their unbelief is a daily, hourly sin; never let them infer from your teaching that they are to be pitied for continuing to make God a liar by rejecting His Son.

Impressed with a sense of their danger, give the ungodly no rest in their sins; knock again and again at the door of their hearts, and knock as for life and death. Your solicitude, your earnestness, your anxiety, your travailing in birth for them, God will bless to their arousing. God works mightily by this instrumentality. But our agony for souls must be real and not feigned, and therefore our hearts must be wrought into true sympathy with God. Low piety means little spiritual power. Extremely pointed addresses may be delivered by men whose hearts are out of order with the Lord, but their result must be small. There is a something in the very tone of the man who has been with Jesus that has more power to touch the heart than the most perfect oratory: remember this and maintain an unbroken walk with God. You will need much night-work in secret if you are to gather many of your Lord's lost sheep. Only by prayer and fasting can you gain power to cast out the worst of devils. Let men say what they will about sovereignty; God connects special success with special states of heart, and if these are lacking, He will not do many mighty works.

45

The Grace of Trouble[1]

"Why has this trouble happened to me?" God has a gracious design in it.

There are many men who are brought to Christ by trouble. Many a sinner has sought the Savior on his sickbed who never would have sought Him anywhere else. Many a merchant whose trade has prospered has lived without God; he has been glad to find the Savior when his house has tottered into bankruptcy. We have known many a person who could afford to despise God while the stream flowed smoothly on, but that same man has been compelled to bow his knee and seek peace through the blood of Christ when he has come into the whirlpool of distress and the whirlwind of trouble has gotten hold upon him.

There is a story told that, in the times of old, Artaxerxes[2] and another great king were engaged in a furious fight. In the middle of the battle a sudden eclipse happened, and such was the horror of all the warriors that they made peace there and then. O if an eclipse of trouble should induce you to ground arms and seek to be reconciled to God! Sinner, you are

---

1. From "The Solar Eclipse," *NPSP*, 4:149–50. A sermon delivered March 14, 1858, at the Music Hall.

2. Artaxerxes was king of Persia from 465 to 424 BC. He is also a central figure in the biblical books of Ezra and Nehemiah.

fighting against God, lifting the arm of your rebellion against Him. Happy shall you be if that trouble that is now fallen upon you should lead you to throw down the weapons of your rebellion and fly to the arms of God and say, "God be merciful to me a sinner."[3] It will be the best thing that you have ever done. Your trouble will be far better to you than joys could have been if your sorrows shall induce you to fly to Jesus, who can make peace through the blood of His cross.

May this be the happy result of your own troubles and sorrows.

But furthermore, eclipses of grace have also their end and design. The Christian asks why it is that God does not seem to favor him in his conscience as much as he did formerly. "Why is it that I have not more faith? Why have the promises lost their sweetness? Why has the Word of God seemed to fail in its power in operating upon my soul? Why has God hidden His face from me?" Christian, it is so that you may begin to search yourself and say, "Shew me wherefore thou contendest with me."[4] God's people are afflicted in order that they may not go astray. "Before I was afflicted," said the psalmist, "I went astray: but now have I kept thy word."[5] Leave a Christian alone, and he becomes like a piece of iron covered with rust; he loses all his brightness. Take the file of affliction, and once more the brightness becomes apparent. Christians without trouble would be like oysters without the sickness; they would not

---

3. Luke 18:13.
4. Job 10:2.
5. Psalm 119:67.

have produced pearls. The pearl oyster would have no pearl unless some disease had fallen upon it, and were it not that trouble lights upon the Christian, he would live without producing the pearl of a holy and contented piety. God's rods are improvers; when they are laid upon us, they always mend us. God searches the Christian, that He may cleanse him of his weeds; He ploughs him deep that He may turn up the subsoil to the air, that the influence of the divine Spirit may rest upon him. He puts us into the crucible and into the furnace, that the heat may burn away our dross and may consume all our impurities. He sends us into the deep waters, that they may be like a sacred baptism to us and may help in sanctifying us by delivering us from our pride, our lust, our worldliness, and our conceit. Happy is the man who understands this—who knows that all things work together for good to them that love God, and believes that even an eclipse of God's countenance has its end and design, in making him perfectly conformed to the image of Christ Jesus the Lord.

46

Enduring Persecution[1]

Did the Church of Rome in more modern times burn one of our glorious reformers—John Huss— yet did not Martin Luther come forward as if the ashes of Huss had begotten Luther? When Wycliffe had passed away, did not the very fact of Wycliffe being persecuted help to spread his doctrines? And were there not found hundreds of young men who in every market town in England read the Lollards'[2] Scriptures and proclaimed the Lollards' faith? And so, depend upon it, it shall ever be. Give a dog a bad name, and you hang him; give a Christian a bad name, and you honor him. Do give to any Christian some ill name, and before long a Christian denomination will take that name to itself, and it will become a title of honor. When George Fox[3] was called "Quaker," it was a strange name—one to laugh at—but those men of God who followed him called themselves Quakers too, and so it lost its reproach. They called the followers of Whitefield and Wesley

---

1. From C. H. Spurgeon, *Words of Wisdom for Daily Living* (Bellingham, Wash.: Logos Bible Software, 2009), 48–50.

2. The Lollards were the followers of John Wycliffe who were known for translating the Scriptures into vernacular English.

3. George Fox (1624–1691) was the founder of the Quaker movement.

"Methodists";[4] they took the title of Methodists, and it became a respectful designation. When many of our Baptist forefathers, persecuted in England, went over to America to find shelter, they imagined that among the Puritans they would have a perfect rest, but Puritan liberty of conscience meant, "The right and liberty to think as they did, but no toleration to those who differed." The Puritans of New England, as soon as ever a Baptist made his appearance among them, persecuted him with as little compunction as the Episcopalians had the Puritans. No sooner was there a Baptist than he was hunted up and brought before his own Christian brethren. Mark you, he was brought up for a fine, for imprisonment, confiscation, and banishment before the very men who had themselves suffered persecution. And what was the effect of this? The effect has been that in America, where we were persecuted, we are the largest body of Christians. Where the fire burnt the most furiously, there the good old Calvinistic doctrine was taught and the Baptist became the more decidedly a Baptist than anywhere else, with the most purity and the least dross. Nor have we ever lost the firmness of our grip upon the fundamental doctrine for which our forefathers stained the baptismal pool with blood by all the trials and persecutions that have been laid upon us, and never shall we.

---

4. George Whitefield (1714–1770) and John Wesley (1703–1791) are considered two of the principle founders of the Methodist movement. Whitefield was the informal leader of the Calvinistic Methodists, while Wesley was the key organizer of the Arminian Methodists. The vast majority of modern Methodists identify more with the latter.

Upon the entire church, at the last, there shall not be even the smell of fire. I see her come out of the furnace. I see her advance up the hill toward her final glory with her Lord and Master, and the angels look at her garments; they are not tattered. Nay, the fangs of her enemies have not been able to make a single rent[5] therein. They draw near to her; they look upon her flowing ringlets, and they are not crisp with heat; they look upon her very feet, and though she has trodden the coals, they are not blistered, and her eyes have not been dried up by the furiousness of the seven times heated flame. She has been made more beautiful, more fair, more glorious by the fires, but hurt she has not been, nor can she be. Turn, then, to the individual Christian, and remember that the promise stands alike firm and fast with each believer. Christian, if you are truly a child of God, your trials cannot destroy you, and what is better still, you can lose nothing by them. You may seem to lose for today, but when the account comes to be settled, you shall not be found to be a farthing[6] the loser by all the temptations of all the world or all the attacks of Satan that you have endured. Nay, more, you shall be wondrously the gainer. Your trials, having worked patience and experience, shall make you rich. Your temptations, having taught you your weakness and shown you where your strength lies, shall make you strong.

---

5. *Rent* is an archaic term meaning "a tear."

6. A *farthing* was a coin in British currency that represented one quarter of a penny. In context, Spurgeon is suggesting that at the end of the age, believers will have lost significantly less than they realized to the world and the devil because of God's grace in their lives.

47

Committing Ourselves to the Father[1]

Learn, next, the duty of prayer. When you are in the very anguish of pain, when you are surrounded by bitter griefs of mind as well as of body, still pray. Drop not the "Our Father."[2] Let not your cries be addressed to the air; let not your moans be to your physician or your nurse, but cry, "Father."

Does not a child so cry when he has lost his way? If he is in the dark at night and he starts up in a lone room, does he not cry out, "Father," and is not a father's heart touched by that cry? Is there anybody here who has never cried to God? Is there one here who has never said "Father"? Then, my Father, put Thy love into their hearts and make them tonight say, "I will arise and go to my father."[3] You shall truly be known to be the sons of God if that cry is in your heart and on your lips.

The next duty is the committal of ourselves to God by faith. Give yourselves up to God, trust yourselves with God. Every morning, when you

---

1. From "Our Lord's Last Cry from the Cross," *MTP*, 39:271–72. A sermon on Luke 23:46 delivered at the Metropolitan Tabernacle on June 9, 1893.

2. This is an allusion to Matthew 6:9, which includes the opening petition of the Lord's Prayer.

3. Luke 15:18.

get up, take yourself, and put yourself into God's custody; lock yourself up, as it were, in the casket of divine protection, and every night, when you have unlocked the box, before you fall asleep, lock it again, and give the key into the hand of Him who is able to keep you when the image of death is on your face. Before you sleep, commit yourself to God; I mean, do that when there is nothing to frighten you, when everything is going smoothly, when the wind blows softly from the south, and the barque[4] is speeding toward its desired haven, still do not make yourself quiet with your own quieting. He who carves for himself will cut his fingers and get an empty plate. He who leaves God to carve for him shall often have fat things full of marrow placed before him. If you can trust, God will reward your trusting in a way that you do not know yet. And then practice one other duty, that of the personal and continual realization of God's presence. "Father, into thy hands I commend my spirit."[5] "Thou art here; I know that Thou art. I realize that Thou art here in the time of sorrow and of danger, and I put myself into Thy hands. Just as I would give myself to the protection of a policeman or a soldier if anyone attacked me, so do I commit myself to Thee, Thou unseen guardian of the night, Thou unwearied keeper of the day. Thou shalt cover my head in the day of battle. Beneath Thy wings I will trust, as a chick hides beneath the hen."

---

4. A *barque* was a type of sailing vessel.
5. Luke 23:46.

See, then, your duty. It is to resign yourself to God, pray to God, commit yourself to God, and rest in a sense of the presence of God. May the Spirit of God help you in the practice of such priceless duties as these!

48

The Dead Who Die in the Lord[1]

That disembodied spirit, clear of spot or blemish, washed and whitened in the blood of the Lamb, passes without fear into the invisible world. It trembles not, though it appears before the eye of justice. No award can come to the forgiven soul except this, "Come, ye blessed of my Father, inherit the kingdom prepared for you."[2] We commit the body of the forgiven sinner to the grave in "sure and certain hope of a joyful resurrection."[3] We give his flesh to be the food of the worm, and his skin may rot to dust, but, though worms destroy his body, yet in his flesh shall he see God,[4] whom his eyes shall see for himself and not another. I was astonished some little time ago

---

1. From "A Cheering Congratulation," *MTP*, 63:257–59. A sermon on Psalm 32:1 delivered at the Metropolitan Tabernacle. This was the final sermon published as part of the New Park Street Pulpit and Metropolitan Tabernacle Pulpit series. In all, the series ran for 63 volumes, including 3,563 sermons spread out over 3,568 individual entries; a few of the sermons were too long to be published as a single entry. See Morden, *Communion with Christ and His People*, 8.

2. Matthew 25:34.

3. This language is taken from the Burial Rite found in the Book of Common Prayer. More than likely, Spurgeon was referencing the 1662 edition, which was used in the Church of England throughout Spurgeon's lifetime.

4. This is an allusion to Job 19:26.

when I heard a good pastor, standing by the coffin of an honored minister, say, "There lies nothing of our brother." Not so, thought I. The bodies of the saints were purchased by Christ; though flesh and blood cannot inherit the kingdom of God, neither can corruption inherit incorruption, yet there will be such a marvelous change pass over the body of the forgiven sinner that the same body changed—but still the same body—shall be reunited with the disembodied spirit to dwell at God's right hand. Hark, hark, the trumpet sounds! Oh! My brethren, we can but speak in prose. These great scenes we shall all of us see. We shall then think after another fashion. The trumpet sounds. The echo reaches heaven. Hell startles at the sound to its lowest domains. This trembling earth is all attention. The sea yields up her dead. A great white cloud comes sailing forth in awful majesty. Upon it there is a throne, where Jesus sits in state. But his heart has no cause to quake whose sins are all forgiven. Well may the ransomed soul be calm amid the pomp and pageantry of that tremendous day, for He who sits upon the throne is the Son of Man, in whose blood we have been washed. Lo! This is the same Jesus who said, "I have forgiven thee."[5] He cannot condemn us. We shall find Him to be our friend whom others find to be their judge. Blessed is that man who is forgiven! See him, as with ten thousand times ten thousand others, pure as himself and like himself, who have washed their robes and made them white in the blood of the Lamb; he ascends to

_____

5. This is not an exact quotation, but likely a free paraphrase of several passages such as Matthew 9:5; Mark 2:5, 9; Luke 5:20, 23; 7:48.

the Celestial City,[6] a perfect man in body and in soul, to dwell forever there! Hark to the acclamations of the ten thousand times ten thousand, the sound of the harpers harping with their harps, and the song that is like great waters.

Write you, write now, "Blessed are the dead which die in the Lord from henceforth: yea, saith the Spirit, that they may rest from their labours; and their works do follow them."[7] But doubly blessed are they then that rise from the dead. Once they were sinners washed in blood, but then, in body and in soul, they shall have come through the precious blood to see Jesus face-to-face.

Oh! How I wish that all of us knew this blessedness! Seek it, friends, seek it. It is to be found. "Seek ye the LORD while he may be found; call ye upon him while he is near."[8] I am especially encouraged in preaching the gospel this evening because I have just been seeing some who have been recently converted. There are hearers of the gospel among you who have been listening to me for many years. Often have I feared that, in your case, I had labored in vain; but I have great hope now concerning some of you. The Lord keeps bringing in the old hearers of eight, nine, and ten years' standing. Oh! I pray the Lord to save every one of you and bring you into the fold. I do long and pant that I may present you all before my Master's face with joy! Even should you go and

---

6. The *Celestial City* is a term used for heaven in John Bunyan's *Pilgrim's Progress*.

7. Revelation 14:13.

8. Isaiah 55:6.

join other churches and serve the Lord elsewhere, that will cause me no sorrow or regret. But God forbid that any of you should despise mercy, reject the gospel, and die in your sins. May you prove the blessedness of pardon, and then shall we meet, an unbroken congregation, before the throne.

The Lord grant it, for His name's sake. Amen.

49

A Gospel Plea[1]

My Dear William,

You see by this address that I am no longer at Mr. Swindell's[2] but am very comfortable here in a smaller school of about fifteen boys. I suppose you are at home but find farming is not all play, nor perhaps altogether so profitable or pleasant as study; it is well said, "We do not know the value of our mercies till we lose them."

Knowing (in some humble measure, at least) the value of religion, let me also bring it before your attention. If you give yourself time to think, you will soon remember that you must die, and if you meditate one more moment, you will recollect that you have a soul and that soul will never die but will live forever, and if you die in your present state, it must live in endless torment. You are an accountable being; God, who made you, demands perfect obedience. But you must own that you have sinned; say not "I am not a great sinner," for one sin only would

---

1. From "The Urgency of Finding Real Religion. A Letter to Master William Cooper. Cambridge, 1851," *Letters of Charles Haddon Spurgeon*, ed. Iain H. Murray (Edinburgh: Banner of Truth, 1992), 67–69.

2. John Swindell was principal of the school Spurgeon attended in Newmarket, Cambridgeshire, in 1849–1850.

be sufficient to sink your soul forever in the pit of perdition. The sentence of death stands against you, and mercy alone stays its execution. Seeing now that you are in such danger, how do you think to escape? Surely you will not be content to die as you are, for you will one day find it no light matter to endure the hot displeasure of an angry God. Do you imagine that, if you live better for the future, God will forgive your past offenses? That is a mistake; see if you can find it in the Bible.

Perhaps you intend to think about religion after you have enjoyed sin a little longer, or (but surely you are not so foolish) possibly you think that you are too young to die. But who knows whether that future time will be afforded, and who said that you can turn to Christ just when you please? Your heart is deceitful above all things and your natural depravity so great that you will not turn to God. Trust not, then, to resolutions made in your own strength; they are but wind; nor to yourself, who are but a broken reed; nor to your own heart, or you are a fool. There is no way of salvation but Christ; you cannot save yourself, having no power even to think one good thought; neither can your parents' love and prayers save you; none but Jesus can. He is the Savior of the helpless, and I tell you that He died for all who feel their vileness and come to Him for cleansing.

You do not deserve salvation; well, there is not a jot of merit on the sinner's part mentioned in the covenant. You have nothing, you are nothing, but Christ is all, and He must be everything to you, or you will never be saved. None reach heaven but by free grace and through free grace alone. Even a faint desire after any good thing came from God, from whom you must get more, for He gives liberally, and no poor sinner, begging at His door, was ever yet sent empty away.

Look at the blessedness of real religion: no one is truly happy but a child of God. The believer is safe, for God has promised to preserve him, and once you have the pearl of great price, it cannot be taken from you. The way to heaven is faith, "looking unto Jesus;"[3] this faith is the gift of God, and none but those who have it know its value. Oh! May you possess it—is the earnest prayer of—

Yours faithfully,

CHARLES H. SPURGEON

---

3. Hebrews 12:2.

Reading Spurgeon

Charles Spurgeon has always been a beloved author among pastors and other Bible teachers, in part because his published writings offer a feast of sermonic material for citation and illustration. Spurgeon himself was the "Prince of Preachers," so most readers should begin with his published sermons. The *New Park Street Pulpit* (6 volumes) and *Metropolitan Tabernacle Pulpit* (63 volumes) have both been reprinted by Pilgrim Press. These volumes are also widely available in searchable electronic form on platforms such as Logos Bible Software. Many sermons selected from the published series are also available on the internet through websites such as The Spurgeon Archive and The Christian Classics Ethereal Library.[1]

In recent years, B&H Academic has begun to publish *The Lost Sermons of C. H. Spurgeon*, based on messages which were first delivered during Spurgeon's Waterbeach pastorate from 1851 to 1854. These sermons, which range from partial manuscripts to

---

1. See Spurgeon's Sermons, The Spurgeon Archives, available online at http://archive.spurgeon.org/, and Spurgeon's Sermons from The Metropolitan Tabernacle Pulpit, Christian Classics Ethereal Library, available online at http://www.iclnet.org/pub/resources/text/history/spurgeon/spurgeon-home.html.

Spurgeon in Study

C. H. Spurgeon, *C. H. Spurgeon's Autobiography. Compiled from His Diary, Letters, and Records.* Vol. 4. 4 vols (London: Passmore and Alabaster, 1900), 289.

simple outlines, have up to this time not been accessible, in part because they were misplaced in the Heritage Room Archives at Spurgeon's College until being rediscovered a few years ago. A team of scholars affiliated with the Spurgeon Library at Midwestern Baptist Theological Seminary are laboring to publish this material. To date, three volumes have been published in both hardcover and handsome collector editions. These volumes are noteworthy because they include far more historical and biographical information, timelines, and scholarly apparatus than the *New Park Street Pulpit* and *Metropolitan Tabernacle Pulpit* series. Yet, despite the level of scholarship being dedicated to this project, the volumes remain accessible to pastors and laypeople.

In addition to the aforementioned series, evangelical publishing houses have periodically published compilations of Spurgeon's sermons. Examples include Zondervan's five-volume *Library of Spurgeon's Sermons* (1977), Baker's four-volume *My Sermon Notes: Charles H. Spurgeon* (1981), Baker's ten-volume *Spurgeon's Sermons* (1987), Kregel's sixteen-volume *C. H. Spurgeon's Sermon Series* (1993–1996), and Hendrickson's five-volume *Spurgeon's Sermons* (1996). Numerous single-volume collections of select Spurgeon sermons have been published over the years, both in print and in electronic form. These books are often organized thematically. Some of the most famous examples of this genre were published shortly after Spurgeon's death in 1892, including *All of Grace* (1892), *Till He Come: Communion Meditations and Addresses* (1896), and *Grace Triumphant* (1904). More recent examples include volumes on prayer, revival, and the doctrines of grace.[2]

Spurgeon wrote many books during his lifetime, and some of them have remained enduringly popular. *Morning by Morning* (1865) and *Evening by Evening* (1868) are devotional works that continue to appeal to evangelical readers. While less popular than the devotional books, *John Ploughman's Talks* (1868) is a helpful resource for those interested in short chapters addressing matters of everyday Christian faithfulness. *The Treasury of David* (1870), Spurgeon's multivolume pastoral commentary on the Psalms, remains enormously popular with pastors and other Bible teachers. Each of these volumes have been reprinted in numerous editions.

Some of Spurgeon's best-known books began as material taught to the students at Spurgeon's College. The most famous book in this genre is probably *Lectures to My Students* (1875), which includes Spurgeon's lectures on the nature of pastoral ministry. The book continues to be widely assigned in seminaries and Bible colleges. The follow-up volume, *Commenting and Commentaries* (1876), focuses on how ministers

---

2. Charles H. Spurgeon, *Spurgeon's Sermons on Prayer* (Peabody, Mass.: Hendrickson, 2007); C. H. Spurgeon, *Sermons on Great Prayers of the Bible* (Peabody, Mass.: Hendrickson, 2015); C. H. Spurgeon, *Revival Year Sermons: Preached at the Surrey Music Hall During 1859* (Edinburgh: Banner of Truth, 1996); and Charles Spurgeon, *Sovereign Grace Pulpit: The Doctrines of Grace from the Sermons of Charles Haddon Spurgeon* (Meeker, Colo.: Sola Scriptura, 2014). These examples are barely scratching the surface of one-volume collections of Spurgeon's sermons, the number of which grows every year due to the advent of electronic self-publishing.

should approach commentaries and other related resources in the preparation of their sermons, and includes Spurgeon's reflections on some of the leading works that were available during his lifetime. *The Soul Winner* (1892), published posthumously, includes Spurgeon's lectures on personal evangelism. Like *Lectures to My Students*, this work also remains very popular with pastors and ministerial students.

Much of Spurgeon's writing during his lifetime was dedicated to his weekly periodical, *The Sword and the Trowel*. Though this material has not been as popular as Spurgeon's sermons and books, in part because it has been reprinted less frequently, *The Sword and the Trowel* is more accessible today than ever before because of electronic platforms such as Logos Bible Software. Select articles are also widely available on the internet via websites such as The Spurgeon Archive. Spurgeon was also a voluminous correspondent. Iain Murray compiled some of that correspondence in *Letters of Charles Haddon Spurgeon*.[3] Spurgeon was also a man of prayer, both public and private, and two different volumes collect Spurgeon's own pulpit prayers from the Metropolitan Tabernacle.[4]

For readers interested in Spurgeon's life, the standard work has long been his *Autobiography*, which Susannah Spurgeon compiled shortly after

3. Iain H. Murray, *Letters of Charles Haddon Spurgeon* (Edinburgh: Banner of Truth, 1991).

4. See C. H. Spurgeon, *The Pastor in Prayer*, 2nd ed. (Edinburgh: Banner of Truth, 2004); and C. H. Spurgeon, *Spurgeon's Prayers: Including Advice on How to Improve Prayer Meetings* (Fearn, Ross-shire, Scotland: Christian Heritage, 2017).

her husband's death. It has been reprinted numerous times, most notably in a two-volume set by Banner of Truth.[5] Numerous biographies of Spurgeon were published in the years shortly after his death. Two of the most notable were those of Holden Pike (1892) and W. Y. Fullerton (1919), both of which have frequently been reprinted.[6] Numerous authors have written biographies of Spurgeon in the last generation, many of which are mentioned in the introductory essay to this volume. Of particular note are the biographies by Iain Murray, Arnold Dallimore, Lewis Drummond, Peter Morden, and Tom Nettles.[7]

Of the more topical works related to Spurgeon's life and thought, noteworthy contributions include Murray's classic work on Spurgeon's opposition to hyper-Calvinism, Steve Miller's work on Spurgeon as a model of spiritual leadership, Zack Eswine's study of Spurgeon and suffering, and Matt Carter and Aaron Ivey's historical novel about Spurgeon

---

5. See C. H. Spurgeon, *Autobiography, Volume 1: The Early Years, 1834–1859* (Edinburgh: Banner of Truth, 1962); and C. H. Spurgeon, *Autobiography, Volume 2: The Full Harvest, 1860–1892* (Edinburgh: Banner of Truth, 1973).

6. See G. Holden Pike, *The Life and Work of Charles Haddon Spurgeon*, 2 vols. (Edinburgh: Banner of Truth, 1991); and W. Y. Fullerton, *Charles H. Spurgeon: A Biography* (Chicago: Moody, 1966).

7. Iain H. Murray, *The Forgotten Spurgeon* (Edinburgh: Banner of Truth, 1978); Arnold Dallimore, *Spurgeon: A New Biography* (Edinburgh: Banner of Truth, 1985); Lewis Drummond, *Charles Spurgeon: Prince of Preachers* (Grand Rapids: Kregel, 1992); Peter Morden, *C. H. Spurgeon: The People's Preacher* (Farnham, Surrey, U.K.: CWR, 2010); and Tom J. Nettles, *Living by Revealed Truth: The Life and Pastoral Theology of Charles Haddon Spurgeon* (Fearn, Ross-shire, Scotland: Christian Focus, 2013).

and Thomas Johnson, the latter of whom was a formerly enslaved African American who trained at Spurgeon's College before becoming a missionary to Africa.[8] A final book worth noting is Ray Rhodes's recent study of Susannah Spurgeon, which is now the standard biography of Spurgeon's remarkable wife.[9] While numerous other works might be of more use to scholars interested in Spurgeon, the aforementioned works are especially helpful for pastors and other readers interested primarily in edification.

---

8. Iain H. Murray, *Spurgeon v. Hyper-Calvinism: The Battle for Gospel Preaching* (Edinburgh: Banner of Truth, 1995); Steve Miller, *C. H. Spurgeon on Spiritual Leadership* (Chicago: Moody, 2003); Zack Eswine, *Spurgeon's Sorrows: Realistic Hope for Those Who Suffer from Depression* (Fearn, Ross-shire, Scotland: Christian Focus, 2015); and Matt Carter and Aaron Ivey, *Steal Away Home: Charles Spurgeon and Thomas Johnson, Unlikely Friends on the Passage to Freedom* (Nashville: B&H, 2017).

9. Ray Rhodes Jr., *Susie: The Life and Legacy of Susannah Spurgeon, Wife of Charles H. Spurgeon* (Chicago: Moody, 2018).